HALLOWED

Also by John Bowker and published by SPCK:
A Year to Live (1991)

❧ *Hallowed Ground*

RELIGIONS AND THE POETRY OF PLACE

JOHN BOWKER

First published in Great Britain 1993
Society for Promoting Christian Knowledge
Holy Trinity Church
Marylebone Road
London NW1 4DU

British Library Cataloguing-in-Publication Data
A catalogue record for this book is available from the
British Library

ISBN 0-281-04669-7

Printed in Great Britain by
The Longdunn Press Ltd, Bristol

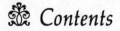 *Contents*

✿ Introduction

With what adventure can we still explore the world? A hundred years ago, much of the map of Africa was still a blank sheet, empty of detail; and Phineas Fogg went round the world in eighty days. A hundred years later, Saloo Chowdury went into the Guinness Book of Records for driving a car around the world in almost exactly half the time; by plane, it can be done in less than a week. It is a different and more familiar world. When Keats, in contrast, searched for some image to convey the impact when he first looked into Chapman's Homer, it was to the startling wonder of new discovery that he appealed:

> . . . Then felt I like some watcher of the skies
>   When a new planet swims into his ken;
> Or like stout Cortez when with eagle eyes
>   He stared at the Pacific – and all his men
> Look'd at each other with a wild surmise –
>   Silent, upon a peak in Darien.

Perhaps, in some distant future, when we no longer simply watch the skies but begin to move among the stars, we will recover something of that childlike, open-mouthed wonder at the novelty of place, so strangely captured in Andrew Marvell's poem, 'Bermudas':

> Where the remote Bermudas ride
> In the ocean's bosom unespied,
> From a small boat, that rowed along,
> The listening winds received this song.

> 'What should we do but sing his praise
> That led us through the watery maze,
> Unto an isle so long unknown,
> And yet far kinder than our own?

Where he the huge sea-monsters wracks,
That lift the deep upon their backs,
He lands us on a grassy stage,
Safe from the storms, and prelate's rage.

He gave us this eternal spring,
Which here enamels everything,
And sends the fowl to us in care,
On daily visits through the air.

He hangs in shades the orange bright,
Like golden lamps in a green night,
And does in the pom'granates close
Jewels more rich than Ormus shows.

He makes the figs our mouths to meet,
And throws the melons at our feet,
But apples plants of such a price,
No tree could ever bear them twice.

With cedars, chosen by his hand,
From Lebanon, he stores the land,
And makes the hollow seas, that roar,
Proclaim the ambergris on shore.

He cast (of which we rather boast)
The gospel's pearl upon our coast,
And in these rocks for us did frame
A temple, where to sound his name.

Oh let our voice his praise exalt,
Till it arrive at heaven's vault:
Which thence (perhaps) rebounding, may
Echo beyond the Mexique Bay.'

    Thus sung they, in the English boat,
An holy and a cheerful note,
And all the way, to guide their chime,
With falling oars they kept the time.

And that explains the purpose of this book, to pick up the
sound of the dipping oars, the cadences, through which
poets are able to make an enterprise out of every voyage of
the mind. To a poet's eye, every excursion into the world,

even to the corner of a familiar street, runs the risk of ambush. Who but a poet would bring London ('the great wen', as Cobbett called it, 'the monster called, "the metropolis of the empire"') under the controlling metaphor of a vision of Jerusalem?

> The fields from Islington to Marybone,
> To Primrose Hill and St John's Wood,
>   Were builded over with pillars of gold,
> And there Jerusalem's pillars stood.
>
>   Her Little-ones ran on the fields,
> The lamb of God among them seen,
>   And fair Jerusalem his Bride,
> Among the little meadows green.
>
>   Pancrass and Kentish-town repose
> Among her golden pillars high,
>   Among her golden arches which
> Shine upon the starry sky.
>
>   The Jew's-harp-house and the Green Man,
> The ponds where Boys to bathe delight,
>   The fields of cows by Willan's farm,
> Shine in Jerusalem's pleasant sight.
>
>   She walks upon our meadows green,
> The Lamb of God walks by her side,
>   And every English Child is seen
> Children of Jesus and his Bride.

But Blake was constrained by other, fundamental metaphors as well – in this case, obviously, by those of Christianity. A purpose of this book is to explore how the poets of different religions and philosophies take us, for that reason, into very different imaginations of place. In a sense, their eyes look on what seem, superficially, to be the same geographies. But they *see* them in entirely different ways. Thomas Hardy made the point that a poet can convert *any* place into consequence, because it is 'a convenient sheet whereon The visions of his mind are drawn':

The blank lack of any charm
Of landscape did no harm:
The bald steep cutting, rigid, rough
And moonlit was enough
For poetry of place.

'Enough', maybe. But 'This world is not conclusion', as Emily Dickinson put it; and those who look, like her, on the world with religious eyes, may well end up by glimpsing even more:

There's a certain Slant of light,
Winter Afternoons –
That oppresses, like the Heft
Of Cathedral Tunes –

Heavenly Hurt, it gives us –
We can find no scar,
But internal difference,
Where the meanings, are –

None may teach it – Any –
'Tis the Seal Despair –
An imperial affliction
Sent us of the Air –

When it comes, the Landscape listens –
Shadows – hold their breath –
When it goes, 'tis like the Distance
On the look of Death –

It is this glimpse of interior meaning which the poetry of place enables us to see. It offers a way of looking through 'the perspective glass' from our particular locations in space and time, so that we begin to see a splendour that might otherwise remain concealed:

By this time the Pilgrims had a desire to go forward, and the Shepherds a desire they should; so they walked together towards the end of the mountains. Then said the Shepherds one to another, Let us here shew to the Pilgrims the gates of the Celestial City, if they have skill to look through our perspective glass. The Pilgrims then lovingly accepted the motion; so they had them to the top of a high hill, called Clear, and gave them their glass to look.

Then they essayed to look, but the remembrance of that last thing that the Shepherds had shewed them, made their hands shake; by means of which impediment, they could not look steadily through the glass; yet they thought they saw something like the gate, and also some of the glory of the place.

The religious poets of place hold our hands steady so that we can look through their glass along the lines of appropriate perspective, until they run together at a distant point of glory and truth.

Lawyers sometimes say in court that they intend to let their witnesses speak for themselves. I have done the same in this book. I have indicated sources where I have been able to do so, but I have not drawn attention to my own poems or translations.

The book is based on programmes originally broadcast on the BBC World Service. It owes everything to the professional acumen of the producer of the programmes, David Craig, and to the unfailing support and hard work of his colleague, Marion Wyatt. In a period of frustrating illness, the book would have made no progress but for Margaret, my wife, to whom it is offered as a 'Thank you' – for that and for much more.

ONE

🎆 Remembered Places

> I remember, I remember,
> The house where I was born,
> The little window where the sun
> Came peeping in at morn . . .

That, for many of us, is where the poetry of place begins, in the recovery of sights and scenes long lost in time:

> I wandered lonely as a cloud
> That floats on high o'er vales and hills,
> When all at once I saw a crowd,
> A host of golden daffodils;
> Beside the lake, beneath the trees,
> Fluttering and dancing in the breeze.

It is all so familiar: the poetry of place becomes the poetry of recollection and recovery:

> For oft when on my couch I lie
> In vacant or in pensive mood,
> They flash upon that inward eye
> Which is the bliss of solitude;
> And then my heart with pleasure fills
> And dances with the daffodils.

It all sounds so innocent and chaste. And yet, not so; for both Thomas Hood and Wordsworth knew how far the interval of life had led them out of Eden: 'Shades of the prison-house begin to close/ Upon the growing boy':

> I remember, I remember,
> The fir trees dark and high;
> I used to think their slender tops
> Were close against the sky:
> It was a childish ignorance,

> But now 'tis little joy
> To know I'm further off from Heav'n
> Than when I was a boy.

It is, therefore, a major part of the *religious* poetry of place that it takes us further into the scene by giving us the eyes, not just of nostalgia, but of connection and involvement. It is *we*, with our own histories and our own exiles from Eden, who are carried by the poetry into these scenes as the places of our lost innocence – but the places also where our redemption and our enlightenment may yet begin. Wordsworth looked back with sorrow on poetry which had captivated him when young but which, as he grew older, had lost its power, its 'never-ending show, with music, incense, festival and flowers!'

> I am sad
> At thought of raptures now for ever flown;
> Almost to tears I sometimes could be sad
> To think of, to read over, many a page,
> Poems withal of name, which at that time
> Did never fail to entrance me, and are now
> Dead in my eyes, dead as a theatre
> Fresh emptied of spectators.

So Wordsworth in *The Prelude*. Yet he was equally clear that it is *only* poetry which can redeem the loss:

> Here we must pause: this only let me add,
> From heart-experience, and in humblest sense
> Of modesty, that he, who in his youth
> A daily wanderer among woods and fields
> With living Nature hath been intimate,
> Not only in that raw unpractised time
> Is stirred to ecstasy, as others are,
> By glittering verse; but further, doth receive,
> In measure only dealt out to himself,
> Knowledge and increase of enduring joy
> From the great Nature that exists in works
> Of mighty poets. Visionary power
> Attends the motions of the viewless winds,
> Embodied in the mystery of words:

There, darkness makes abode, and all the host
Of shadowy things work endless changes there,
As in a mansion like their proper home.
Even forms and substances are circumfused
By that transparent veil with light divine,
And, through the turnings intricate of verse,
Present themselves as objects recognised,
In flashes, and with glory not their own.

In this way, the poetry of place becomes also the poetry of praise: it refuses to relinquish or despise those sudden glimpses of glory. Few people exemplify this more clearly than Gerard Manley Hopkins. Over many years, he developed, from the thirteenth century philosophy of Duns Scotus, the belief that all things bear the inward stress of their own God-given meaning – what he called, not landscape, but 'inscape'. 'No doubt', he wrote to Robert Bridges in 1879, 'my poetry errs on the side of oddness. I hope in time to have a more balanced and Miltonic style. But as air, melody, is what strikes me most of all in music, and design in painting, so design, pattern, or what I am in the habit of calling "inscape" is what I above all aim at in poetry.' 'Inscape' lies in the particularity of things to be quintessentially what they are, and not other, as William Lynch has summarized the point:

> To use familiar examples, the finite is given metaphysical form in the concept of *haecceitas*, the pure and absolute *thisness*-and-not-thatness which the great Scotus saw in all things; in the 'inscape' which Hopkins, following in Scotus' footsteps, saw in everything; in the single farthing of the Gospel, which was the key to salvation; and in the little, sensible things which were the source of insight for St Thomas.

What Scotus meant by the discernment of *haecceitas* can be seen in his Oxford Commentary on the *Sentences* of Peter Lombard:

> By grasping just what things are of themselves, a person separates the essences from the many additional incidental

features associated with them in the sense-image, and sees what is true . . . as a more universal truth.

Hopkins read the Commentary in 1872, and at once 'the great Scotus' became entangled in Hopkins's memory of his own time at Oxford, as he tried to realize in poetry what Scotus, also in Oxford, had glimpsed as a philosopher:

> Towery city and branchy between towers;
> Cuckoo-echoing, bell-swarmèd, lark-charmèd, rock-
> racked, river-rounded,
> The dapple-eared lily below thee; that country and town
> did
> Once encounter in, here coped and poisèd powers;
>
> Thou hast a base and brickish skirt there, sours
> That neighbour-nature thy grey beauty is grounded
> Best in; graceless growth, thou hast confounded
> Rural rural keeping – folk, flocks, and flowers.
>
> Yet ah! this air I gather and I release
> He lived on; these weeds and waters, these walls are
> what
> He haunted who of all men most sways my spirits to
> peace;
>
> Of realty the rarest-veinèd unraveller; a not
> Rivalled insight, be rival Italy or Greece;
> Who fired France for Mary without spot.

In 1874, Hopkins was sent to St Beuno's in North Wales, and there, seized by the beauty of the Clwyd valley, his theory took off into celebration. The wearying smudge of human error and sin is not ignored, but the hope of glory begins once more to shine:

> The world is charged with the grandeur of God,
>   It will flame out, like shining from shook foil;
>   It gathers to a greatness, like the ooze of oil
> Crushed. Why do men then now not reck his rod?
> Generations have trod, have trod, have trod;
>   And all is seared with trade; bleared, smeared with
>   toil;

And wears man's smudge and shares man's smell:
the soil
Is bare now, nor can foot feel, being shod.
And for all this, nature is never spent;
There lives the dearest freshness deep down things;
And though the last lights off the black West went
Oh, morning, at the brown brink eastward, springs –
Because the Holy Ghost over the bent
World broods with warm breast and with ah! bright
wings.

But as well as the real presence of the Holy Ghost in
Wales, Hopkins knew also the places where the absence of
God seemed equally clear. The places where he subsequently
lived – Liverpool and Ireland – were a heavy burden upon
him:

To seem the stranger lies my lot, my life
Among strangers. Father and mother dear,
Brothers and sisters are in Christ not near
And he my peace / my parting, sword and strife.

England, whose honour O all my heart woos, wife
To my creating thought, would neither hear
Me, were I pleading, plead nor do I: I wear-
y of idle a being but by where wars are rife.

I am in Ireland now; now I am at a third
Remove. Not but in all removes I can
Kind love both give and get. Only what word

Wisest my heart breeds dark heaven's baffling ban
Bars or hell's spell thwarts. This to hoard unheard,
Heard unheeded, leaves me a lonely began.

But in contrast to the lonely failures, as he thought them,
of his last years, he continued to be sustained by that place
in North Wales, where he knew that he was much *closer* to
heaven than when he was a boy: 'I remember, I remember';
and he went there in memory to be repaired:

I remember a house where all were good
  To me, God knows, deserving no such thing:
  Comforting smell breathed at very entering,
Fetched fresh, as I suppose, off some sweet wood.
That cordial air made those kind people a hood
  All over, as a bevy of eggs a mothering wing
  Will, or mild nights the new morsels of Spring:
Why, it seemed of course; seemed of right it should.

Lovely the woods, waters, meadows, combes, vales,
All the air things wear that build this world of Wales;
  Only the inmate does not correspond:

God, lover of souls, swaying considerate scales,
Complete thy creature dear O where it fails,
  Being mighty a master, being a father and fond.

The poetry of place, therefore, has this power to make us, not simply travellers in space, but travellers in time as well. It creates the possibility of our healing and of our hope – first, because it renews the days of our peace; but second also, because it can take us back to the places of our hurt in the past, and there, through the cleansing of our memory, it can start the process of our completion and cure. In that way it creates in us a better chance by far of becoming a hood of care and protection for others.

TWO

❀ China and Tao

Hopkins sought the 'inscape' of the places where he lived. In his poetry, that was what he attempted to convey, not the more obvious description of what lay before his eyes. But *what* was he discerning within the poetry of place? A Chinese poet would have had little difficulty in giving an answer:

> You look at it, but it is not to be seen;
>   Its name is Formless.
> You listen to it, but it is not to be heard;
>   Its name is Soundless.
> You grasp it, but it is not to be held;
>   Its name is Bodiless.
> These three elude all scrutiny,
>   And hence they blend and become one.

But what is the 'It'? It is here that China goes off in a very different direction from Hopkins, because the 'It' is the Tao. And what is the Tao?

> The Tao that can be described is not the eternal Tao;
> the name that can be named is not the eternal name:
> nameless, it is the origin of earth and heaven;
> able to be named, it is the mother of all things.

So begins the famous *Tao-te Ching*, a deep well of living water for Chinese thought and life – obscurely so, at first sight: for how can we draw much inspiration from that of which we cannot speak? 'Whereof one cannot speak', observed Wittgenstein, 'Thereof one must be silent'. But since the Tao is the source, the unproduced producer, of all that is – the reason why anything exists at all – the Tao is not *wholly* indiscernible. All that exists is a consequence of Tao; almost, as we might say, of primordial energy, of particles and atoms hurtling into new architectures of appearance – plants and planets, or stars and suns. The Tao, the Source, cannot be found as one object among other objects in the universe; rather, it supplies the possibility of all nature and of all individual appearances; but those are the Tao as it becomes nameable:

> Always non-existent, that we may apprehend its inner secret,
> Always existent, that we may discern its outer manifestations:
> These two are the same;
> Only as they manifest themselves do they receive different names.

The outer appearance of things, though often beautiful and fair, is only the surface of truth: to look *at* it is to stand in a doorway and admire the timber and its construction, while never passing through the doorway into life:

> Leave, leave, thy gadding thoughts;
>   Who pores
>   And spies
>   Still out of doors
>   Descries
> Within them nought.

> The skin, and shell of things
>   Though fair,
>   Are not
>   Thy wish nor prayer
>   But got
> By mere despair
>   Of wings.

> To rack old elements,
>   Or dust
>   And say
>   Sure here he must
>   Needs stay
> Is not the way,
>   Nor just.

> Search well another world; who studies this,
> Travels in clouds, seeks manna, where none is.

With almost all of that, written though it was by a Christian poet, the Chinese Taoist would agree. Where he would not agree would be in the advice to search well *another* world: the Tao can be found by searching well *this* world, and not least, as we shall see, by travelling in clouds.

If, then, we ask, 'Who will give us the wings to fly through the doorway of sense and perception in order to find the Truth which is, and which is the source of all being and all appearance?', the Chinese have no doubt: the answer is the poet, and with the poet the painter. For poetry in China is called 'the host' and painting 'the guest': poetry invites the painter to unfold the truth which poetry discerns and tries to mediate to us.

And what is that truth? It is the realization that we are not other than the Tao, the primordial Source, which builds us, as we would say, of atoms and molecules, as it does all other appearances around us. Thus the simplest way to realize the truth of our own nature is to realize that we are not other than those appearances: we and they are equally the manifestation of Tao; we, with the mountains and the trees, are the Tao as it becomes nameable and existent. We flow into nature because it is not other than ourselves, and we return from it to ourselves, in a deep innocence and peace – what the Chinese call 'the inner joy of the poet':

> Near the middle of the day, when clouds are thin and the breeze is light,
> I stroll along the river, passing the willows and the budding trees.
> People of the day do not understand my inner joy;
> They say I am idling around like all the young people of today.

So the place of poetry for the Chinese is supremely the mountain – the place of isolation where earth and heaven touch and merge in clouds and mist:

> You ask me why I stay in these blue mountains.
> I smile, but I do not answer.
> O, my mind is at ease!

Peach blossoms and flowing streams pass without a
   trace:
How different from the ordinary world!

Different, yes: but not detached *from* the ordinary world.
The Emperor Hui Tsung, of the Sung dynasty, used to set
exams for those aspiring to enter official employment.
He would set a line of poetry and require the candidate
to paint an illustration of the line. On one occasion he set
the line, 'A monastery buried deep in the mountains'. The
winning scroll portrayed the minute figure of a monk
collecting water from a stream: there was no monastery
depicted in the painting; yet by inference the monastery
must be somewhere near, for why else would a monk
be collecting water in the mountains? If we are to discern
the Tao, then both painter and poet must leave out far more
than they put in, since otherwise the eye is distracted
by detail from discerning the truth – that inner pulse
of being. A poem, therefore (as Archibald Macleish was
to put it in another tradition), must 'be' rather than
portray:

A poem should be equal to:
Not true

For all the history of grief
An empty doorway and a maple leaf

For love
The leaning grasses and two lights
above the sea –

A poem should not mean
But be.

For that reason, Chinese poets could find peace and
inspiration in places, like mountains, which for others might
have seemed full of threat and danger:

Wave-break of ridge and peak
From near or far, from foot or summit,
The form flows.
The Lu mountains have no face

Available for recognition,
Once we ourselves
Are drowned in their depth.

That kind of poetry of place was being written at a time
when Europeans were still regarding mountains as places
of desolation and danger. In his book, *The Lakers*, Norman
Nicholson, the Lakeland poet, recorded the long process
through which the mountains were discovered in the West
as places of beauty and of recreation.

The Middle Ages had seen the village as a tiny clearing of
order among the illimitable wildness of nature; the
seventeenth century saw the mountains as the last
defiance of disorder among the colonies of civilization.
These dark woods and mountains were to them as was
the first chaos to God; England had her Newton, so let
her now have light. At this time travel, instead of being
discouragingly dangerous and laborious, began to look
almost as if it might become a pleasure. Highway
robbery was decreasing, roads were improving; turnpikes
were opened. The time was right for the exploration of
England and the discovery of the Lakes.

Even then, mountains remained, in the Western imagination,
places of obdurate resistance, as they were for Rilke:

Maybe through heavy mountains I am wending,
in hard enveinings, like an ore, alone;
and am so deep that I can see no ending
and no horizon: all in nearness blending,
and all that nearness turned to stone.

Anguish I'm still so far from comprehending,
and that's why this great darkness makes me small;
if, though, it's *You*, get heavy, smash the wall,
that your whole hand on me may be descending,
and you with my whole cry I may befall.

Yet through all this period, poets in China were finding
mountains to be places of profound enlightenment:

Since the days of my middle life
I was deeply devoted to Tao.
Recently I came to live
In the mountains of Chung-nan.
Often, with joy in my heart,
I wander alone from here to here.
It is a wonderful thing
To know myself as I am.
When the streams end my journey
I settle down and catch
The moment of rising mists.

Wang Wei, who wrote that in the fifth century CE, did more than almost any other figure to unify the arts of poetry and painting in China – because he knew at first hand the inner joy of union with all being, and its peace.

Lately I became aware of the meaning of still peace.
Day after day I stayed away from the crowd.
I cleaned my cottage and prepared it for the visit of a monk
Who came to me from the distant mountains.
He descended from the cloud-hidden peaks
To see me in my thatched house.
Sitting on the grass we shared the resin of the pine;
Burning incense, we read the words of Tao.
When the day was over, we lit our lamp.
The temple bells announced the beginning of the evening.
In a moment I realised the still peace which is most certain joy,
And I felt that my life has infinite space.

That is not the poetry of description: it is the poetry of participation, of realizing truth within the least atoms which construct this brief appearance of a body. And if we ourselves do not belong to that tradition, then this at least we can gain from it, that we try each day to practise this sympathy of sense, by which we begin to feel – not think, but feel – this deep identity of shared and common being, with the street and the car and the cornflakes, with our family, our neighbour and our colleagues at work, however awkward or difficult they may be; and this, if we attempt it with good faith, will most certainly create the inner joy of the poet, and the space where those 'people of the day' cannot break through and steal.

THREE

✿ Traherne

In places of isolated nature, like the mountains, the poets of China discovered what they called 'an inner joy'. So too did Traherne, the seventeenth-century Christian poet, for whom not just the mountains but the whole world was a place of paradise – especially if it is seen through the recovered eyes of childhood, the eyes of primordial innocence which delivered to Traherne 'those Paul and Virgin Apprehensions which I had in my infancy':

> Certainly Adam in Paradise had not more sweet and curious apprehensions of the world than when I was a child. All appeared new, and strange at the first, inexpressibly rare, and delightful and beautiful. I was a little stranger which at my entrance into the world was saluted and surrounded with innumerable joys. . . . All time was eternity and a perpetual Sabbath. Is it not strange, that an infant should be heir of the world, and see those mysteries which the books of the learned never unfold? . . . The corn was orient and immortal wheat, which never should be reaped, nor was ever sown. I thought it had stood from everlasting to everlasting. The dust and stones of the street were as precious as gold. The gates were at first the end of the world, the green trees when I saw them first through one of the gates transported and ravished me; their sweetness and unusual beauty made my heart to leap, and almost mad with ecstasy, they were such strange and wonderful thing. The men! O what venerable and reverend creatures did the aged seem! Immortal cherubims! And young men glittering and sparkling angels, and maids strange seraphic pieces of life and beauty! Boys and girls tumbling in the street, and playing, were moving jewels. I knew not that they were born or should die. But all

things abided eternally as they were in their proper places. Eternity was manifest in the light of the day, and some thing infinite behind every thing appeared: which talked with my expectation and moved my desire.

Traherne is the poet of ecstatic joy – the words 'bliss', 'glory', 'felicity', 'good' and 'joy' are all common and recurrent in his poems:

> O! what would I
> Diseased, wanting, melancholy, give
> To find what is felicity,
>   The place where bliss doth live?
>   The regions fair
> Which are not lodg'd in sea nor air,
> Nor woods, nor fields, nor arbour yields, nor springs,
> Nor hev'ns shew to us below, nor kings.
>
>   I might have gon
> Into the city, market, tavern, street,
> Yet only change my station,
>   And strove in vain to meet
>   That eas of mind
> Which all alone I long'd to find:
> A common inn doth no such thing betray,
> Nor doth it walk in people's talk, or play.
>
>   O Eden fair!
> Where shall I seek the soul of holy joy
> Since I to find it here despair;
>   Nor in the shining day,
>   Nor in the shade,
> Nor in the field, nor in a trade
> I can it see? Felicity! O where
> Shall I thee find to eas my mind! O where!

Traherne's answer to himself – the key to ecstasy – is to see the beauties and delights of this self-evident world, and then to see through them into something more, as a child so easily can. What other worlds can we glimpse, as a child does, in reflections – or 'Shadows in the Water'?

In unexperienc'd infancy
Many a sweet mistake doth ly:
Mistake tho false intending true;
A *seeming* somewhat more than *view*;
　　That doth instruct the mind
　　In things that ly behind,
And many secrets to us show
Which afterwards we come to know.

Thus did I by the water's brink
Another world beneath me think;
And while the lofty spacious skies
Reverséd there abus'd my eyes,
　　I fancy'd other feet
　　Came mine to touch and meet;
As by some puddle I did play
Another world within it lay.

Beneath the water people drown'd.
Yet with another Hev'n crown'd
In spacious regions seem'd to go
Freely moving to and fro:
　　In bright and open space
　　I saw their very face;
Eyes, hands and feet they had like mine;
Another sun did with them shine.

'Twas strange that people there should walk,
And yet I could not hear them talk:
That throu a little watry chink,
Which one dry ox or horse might drink,
　　We other worlds should see,
　　Yet not admitted be;
And other confines there behold
Of light and darkness, heat and cold.

I call'd them oft, but call'd in vain;
No speeches we could entertain:
Yet did I there expect to find
Som other world, to please my mind.
　　I plainly saw by these
　　A new Antipodes,

Whom, tho they were so plainly seen,
A film kept off that stood between.

* * *

O ye that stand upon the brink,
Whom I so near me, throu the chink,
With wonder see: what faces there,
Whose feet, whose bodies, do ye wear?
   I my companions see
   In you, another me.
They seeméd others, but are we;
Our second selves those shadows be.

* * *

Of all the play-mates which I knew
That here I do the image view
In other selves; what can it mean?
But that below the purling stream
   Some unknown joys there be
   Laid up in store for me;
To which I shall, when that thin skin
Is broken, be admitted in.

The senses, then, which look upon the places of beauty in this world, are ambassadors who bring us news of a foreign country – 'News from a forrein country came, | As if my treasure and my wealth lay there.' But the messages which they bring require thought to be appreciated; if they fall simply on the surface of the eye, they remain without meaning:

To *walk* abroad is, not with Eys,
But Thoughts, the Fields to see and prize;
   Els may the silent Feet,
      Like Logs of Wood,
Mov up and down, and see no Good,
   Nor Joy nor Glory meet.

Ev'n Carts and Wheels their place do change,
But cannot see; tho very strange
   The Glory that is by:

Dead Puppets may
Mov in the bright and glorious Day,
　Yet not behold the Sky.

And are not Men than they more blind,
Who having Eys yet never find
　The Bliss in which they mov:
　　Like Statues dead
They up and down are carriéd,
　Yet neither see nor lov.

To *walk* is by a Thought to go;
To mov in Spirit to and fro;
　To mind the Good we see;
　　To taste the Sweet;
Observing all the things we meet
　How choice and rich they be.

To note the Beauty of the Day,
And golden Fields of Corn survey;
　Admire the pretty Flow'rs
　　With their sweet Smell;
To prais their Maker, and to tell
　The marks of his great pow'rs.

To fly abroad like activ Bees,
Among the Hedges and the Trees,
　To cull the Dew that lies
　　On evry Blade,
From evry Blossom; till we lade
　Our *Minds*, as they their *Thighs*.

Observ those rich and glorious things,
The Rivers, Meadows, Woods, and Springs,
　The fructifying Sun;
　　To note from far
The Rising of each Twinkling Star
　For us his Race to run.

A little Child these well perceivs,
Who, tumbling among Grass and Leaves,
　May Rich as Kings be thought,

> But there's a Sight
> Which perfect Manhood may delight,
>   To which we shall be brought.
>
> While in those pleasant Paths we talk
> 'Tis *that* tow'rds which at last we walk;
>   But we may by degrees
>   Wisely proceed
> Pleasures of Lov and Prais to heed,
>   From viewing Herbs and Trees.

This 'viewing', this way of seeing, then converts the world to constant opportunity of splendour:

You never enjoy the world aright, till you see how a sand exhibiteth the wisdom and power of God: and prize in evry thing the service which they do you, by manifesting his glory and his goodness to your soul, far more than the visible beauty on their surface, or the material services which they can do your body. . . . Your enjoyment of the world is never right, till evry morning you awake in heaven: see your self in your father's palace: and look upon the skies and the earth and the air, as celestial joys . . . . You never enjoy the world aright, till the sea itself floweth in your veins, till you are clothed with the heavens, and crowned with the stars . . . . Till your Spirit filleth the whole world, and the stars are your jewels, till you are as familiar with the ways of God in all ages as with your walk and table; till you are acquainted with that shady nothing out of which the world was made: till you love men so as to desire their happiness, with a thirst equal to the zeal of your own: till you delight in God for being good to all: you never enjoy the world . . . . Yet further, you never enjoy the world aright, till you so love the beauty of enjoying it, that you are covetous and earnest to persuade others to enjoy it; and so perfectly hate the abominable corruption of men in despising it, that you had rather suffer the flames of hell than willingly be guilty of their error, there is so much blindness and ingratitude and damned folly in it. The world is a mirror of infinite beauty, yet no man sees it. It is a temple of majesty, yet no man regards it. It is a region of light and peace, did not men disquiet it. It is the paradise of God . . . . It is the place of angels, and the gate of heaven.

Traherne is telling us that we are all gifted children: we have received all things as gift, including the very fact that we exist at all:

> These little limbs,
>   These eys and hands which here I find,
> This panting heart wherwith my life begins;
>   Where have ye been? Behind
> What curtain were ye from me hid so long!
> Where was, in what abyss, my new-made tongue?
>
>   When silent I
>   So many thousand thousand years
> Beneath the dust did in a chaos lie,
>   How could I smiles, or tears,
> Or lips, or hands, or eyes, or ears perceiv?
> Welcome ye treasures which I now receiv.
>
>   I that so long
>   Was nothing from eternity,
> Did little think such joys as ear and tongue
>   To celebrate or see:
> Such sounds to hear, such hands to feel, such feet,
> Such eys and objects, on the ground to meet.
>
>   New burnisht joys!
>   Which finest gold and pearl excell!
> Such sacred treasures are the limbs of boys
>   In which a soul doth dwell:
> Their organized joints and azure veins
> More wealth include than the dead world conteins.
>
>   From dust I rise
>   And out of nothing now awake,
> These brighter regions which salute mine eys,
>   A gift from God I take:
> The earth, the seas, the light, the lofty skies,
> The sun and stars are mine; if these I prize.

> Long time before
> I in my mother's womb was born,
> A God preparing did this glorious store,
>   The world for me adorne.
> Into this Eden so divine and fair,
> So wide and bright, I com his son and heir.
>
>   A stranger here,
>   Strange things doth meet, strange glory see,
> Strange treasures lodg'd in this fair world appear,
>   Strange all and new to me:
> But that they *mine* should be who nothing was,
> That strangest is of all; yet brought to pass.

Traherne, therefore, did not seek, as did the Chinese poets, to find his own identity with the Tao, the source of all appearance. He regarded all appearance, including himself within it, as a miraculous gift; but if a gift, then there must be One who gives it; and the Giver remains distinguished from the gift, to be praised in thanksgiving for ever. And if we ourselves do not belong to that tradition, then this at least we can gain from it, that we try to accept the giftedness of ourselves and of all that comes to us. In that way, the chances are good that we in turn will become a living act of praise and a gift of goodness to all whom we will meet each day.

FOUR

🎗 Basho
and the Japanese Haiku

In China, poetry and painting are at one, the host and the guest. Both are marked for excellence, not by what they put in, but by what they leave out. That is why you will rarely see a shadow in a Chinese painting, even when the sun or the moon are clearly evident, for Chinese paintings are not attempting to represent, or re-present, a scene realistically, as a photograph might attempt to do; they are trying to convey that inner identity and unity of all nature and appearance, and this can more effectively be done by allusive suggestion than by reproduction of the superficial appearance. On another occasion when the same emperor Hui Sung (p. 10) set the exam for his would-be civil servants, the line of poetry which he chose for them to illustrate was this: 'When I returned from trampling on flowers, the hoofs of my horse were fragrant.' The winning painting portrayed no meadows full of flowers: the horse is walking on a path, but with two butterflies fluttering round its hoofs: the meadows and the flowers must be somewhere near, but they are not directly visible.

Chinese poets in general were as capable as, say, Wordsworth, of writing the poetry of place in directly descriptive terms – including a description of their own emotions and feelings:

Up and up, the Incense-burner Peak!
In my heart is stored what my eyes and ears perceived.
All the year – detained by official business;
Today at last I got a chance to go.
Grasping the creepers, I clung to dangerous rocks;
My hands and feet – weary with groping for hold.
There came with me three or four friends,
But two friends dared not go further.
At last we reached the topmost crest of the Peak;
My eyes were blinded, my soul rocked and reeled.

The chasm beneath me – ten thousand feet;
The ground I stood on, only a foot wide.
If you have not exhausted the scope of seeing and
    hearing,
How can you realise the wideness of the world?
The waters of the River looked narrow as a ribbon,
P'en Castle smaller than a man's fist.
How it clings, the dust of the world's halter!
It chokes my limbs; I cannot shake it away.
Thinking of retirement, I heaved an envious sigh;
Then, with lowered head, came back to the Ant's Nest.

But in contrast to direct description, the Taoist poet was
more inclined to move in the direction of exclusion, in a way
that goes far beyond even Ruth Pitter's advice about poetry
to Ann Rendall: *'Look at each adjective* severely: an adjective has
no business to be there unless it is striking – it can make a
line or ruin it.' But the severity of the Taoist poet is a knife
to cut through the outward appearance in order to
penetrate to the inner meaning.

Yet if China went far in the poetry of exclusion, Japan
went even further:

Kiyotaki ya	Clear cascades
Nami ni chirikomu	Into the waves scatter
Aomatsuba.	Blue pine-needles.

That is a classic example of the *haiku*. The *haiku* came into
being because the much earlier form of Japanese verse, the
waka, was highly formal and was admired for its skill in
emulating the way such poetry had been written in the
past. Poetry for the people was then rescued in what is
known as *renga*, the linked verse which puts two halves
together in what often proved to be great communal
entertainment. Yet even *renga* developed into rule-bound
sophistication, and poetry began to disappear once more
into an intellectual reservation, far out of the reach of
ordinary people. At that point, what James Reeve once
called 'the idiom of the people' was reinstated through the
development of the *haikai*, the 'free' or 'light-hearted' verse.
That certainly retained the characteristic of the linked

verse, but in content it scarcely met the expectations of more polite society:

| *Nigangigashiku mo* | Bitter, bitter it was |
| *Okashikarikeri* | And yet somehow funny: |

Ware oya no	Even when
Shinuru toki ni mo	My father lay dying
He wo kokite	I went on farting.

Into this contested situation came Basho (1644–94), the original Batman. He described himself as 'neither priest nor layman, bird nor rat, but something flitting about in the middle'. He had begun life as a Samurai, but was then attracted by Buddhism. The fusion of the two can be seen in his combining the buddha-nature (which can be discerned, somewhat like the Tao, in all appearances) with the cherry-blossom (which is the supreme epitome, among the Samurai, of transience and the acceptance of death). In the words of a famous proverb, 'Among flowers it is the cherry-blossom, among men it is the Samurai: the blossom falls in full bloom, and the Samurai accepts death in the midst of life without fear.' So Basho:

| *Kuromite takaki* | Sombre and tall |
| *Kashi no ki no mori* | The forest of oaks |

Saku hana ni	In and out
Chiisaki mon wo	Through the little gate
Detsu iritsu.	To the cherry blossoms.

That remains an example of linked-verse; but Basho took one link only and developed it into the independent form which became known as the *haiku*. The *haiku* is an even more extreme form of compression, made up of three lines of only seventeen syllables: 5, 7, 5. A *haiku* is judged to be successful, partly by its skill in observing the discipline of rule and method, that single most important condition of enduring art; and partly also by the subtlety with which it observes the conventions of content – for example, of *ki*, or 'season'. A *kigo*, or 'seaon word', may be direct, but far more often it is allusive and implied. In these ways, a successful *haiku* becomes a kind of microcosm, a representation in miniature of the whole truth about its subject matter, and therefore of the truth which lies behind *every* subject matter. Every place becomes the occasion of poetry, and poetry is the occasion of truth:

Ishiyama no	White shines the stone
ishi yori shiroshi	Of the mountain rock: whiter yet
aki no kaze.	The autumn wind.

In search of place as the occasion of insight, Basho travelled constantly throughout Japan. He was greeted on his travels much like a pop star being mobbed for his fame. His diary of his journeys, *Nozarishi kiko*, is so called from the first line of its first *haiku*, 'Nozarishi wo', 'In a field of bones exposed to the weather': not surprisingly, therefore, even his last poem sees him journeying still in the mind when his body can no longer move to new places of inspiration:

Tabi ni yande	Stricken on a journey
Yume wa kareno wo	My dreams through withered fields
Kake meguru.	Go wandering still.

It was this 'truth in simplicity', itself a consequence of disciplined intelligence, which so impressed van Gogh, and was converted by him into the painting of place:

> If we study Japanese art, we see a man who is undoubtedly wise, philosophic and intelligent, who spends his time doing – what? In studying the distance between the earth and the moon? No. In studying Bismarck's policy? No. He studies a single blade of grass. But this blade of grass leads him to draw every plant and then the seasons, the wide aspects of the countryside, then animals, then the human figure. So he passes his life, and life is too short to do the whole. Come now, isn't it almost a true religion which these simple Japanese teach us, who live in nature as though they themselves were flowers?

All can be seen in the shape and glaze of a vase or of a plate. At one level, a plate mediates, like a deacon, between kitchen and table; but at another, it mediates the infinite, compressed into a point:

> Looking on light
> in a still point turning
> in a blue glaze
> seizing a swathe of the sky's
> blue glaze
> turning in a still point
> leading to light.

And if we ourselves do not belong to that tradition, then this at least we can learn from it, 'to follow nature', as Basho put it, 'and befriend the four seasons. In whatever you see, behold the flower; in whatever you think, think the moon. Those to whom a form is not a flower are savages; those whose thoughts are not the moon are wild beasts. Forsake the savage! Abandon the beast! Follow nature and return to it':

Haru mo yaya	Spring too, very soon!
keshiki totonou	they are setting the scene for it –
tsuki to ume.	the plum tree and moon.

This penetration of the obvious does not require any great heroic gesture, but a quiet attention to the detail of a particular moment, in order to see through it into truth:

> A man that looks on glass,
> On it may stay his eye;
> Or if he pleaseth, through it pass,
> And then the heaven espy.

What that involves is extremely simple: it is that we cultivate a deliberate sensitivity to the allusive and unexpected value in the least and most trivial of our encounters; for by that endeavour, our lives will be immeasurably enriched, and they will certainly become more humorous: write your epic on an envelope, and the insight will be all the sharper for its abbreviation:

> When I pulled the cork
> from the bottle of Chianti
> I threw away the undergarment
> of straw wrapped around it.

So it stands now in the cold tomb
of the refrigerator
quite naked
unashamed
shivering deliciously.

FIVE

❦ The Qur'an and the Sufis

For the Japanese, the hills are alive, not with the sound of music, but with the pulse of the *kami*. The *kami* is the spirituality inherent in all places and in all things. Nothing can be exhaustively described or accounted for simply by analysing its material parts. Places have power, as equally do animals and humans, to move us and affect us, and it is this power which the Japanese regard as the consequence of *kami*. Mountains, seas, rivers, rocks and trees, in all these *kami* can be encountered – and also worshipped for what they are.

It seems a long way from Islam, where the worship of anything apart from God is a frightening error, to be punished, after death, in fire. And yet, for Muslims, everything in the natural world is equally a sign of God:

> Do not they who doubt the truth
> See the skies above,
> How we made them, and arrayed them,
> Without fault or flaw?
> And the earth, how wide we spread it,
> Setting mountains rooted firm,
> And within it fruitful growing,
> Beautiful in form?
> And we send down
> From the heavens
> Rain with blessing charged;
> From it we produce the gardens,
> And the harvest grain,
> And the lofty palm-trees stretching
> All with shoots of growth,
> These to nourish the servants of God
> With life from a lifeless land:
> So will be the Resurrection
> [Like that will be the going forth from the grave.]

That last phrase, *kadhalik al-khuruj*, 'like that will be the going forth from the grave', shows how all the places of nature, the mountain, the oasis, the grain-fields, are signs pointing to the power of God to create life out of death – as they are signs also to remind us that death is the condition of life:

> Day after day, the wind carries away a rose from the garden: and the heart of the nightingale feels a new sorrow.
>
> The law of time is the same for all: murmur not, and submit to its justice.
>
> The falcon of death carries off, like a pigeon in his talons, all things that are born.
>
> O friend! Set not your heart on this world: for peace undisturbed is not possible here.
>
> The tulip and hyacinth that blossom come from the earth: perhaps from the dust of a face that was lovely, with hair of a hyacinth scent.
>
> Nothing has ever been built on the earth: that time has not changed its perfection.
>
> Yesterday the garden and its flowers: felt the gladness of the jubilant birds.
>
> Today the thorns alone remain: as if never a rose had bloomed in the garden.
>
> This world is a bridge that leads to eternity: the wise build not their home upon the bridge.

So the poetry of place in Islam, not least in the Qur'an, is the poetry of perception – the perceiving of the signs, the *ayat* in Arabic, of God. But that word, *ayat*, is also the word for the verses of the Qur'an, the sublime and greatest poetry for Muslims because it comes from God. It is mediated as revelation through a prophet, but he is not the author of it. In the Qur'an, therefore, place and poetry merge: they are both, in their own way, signs pointing to God: 'God makes clear to you his signs, that you may perhaps reflect, in this life and in the next' (s.ii.217).

That is why the great Sufi poets, the mystical poets of Islam, could see even themselves, in their ecstatic union of love with God, as outposts of God in the world, as living signs of his creative act:

We are the flute, the music you,
The mountain we, which echoes you,
The chessmen set in line by you,
To win or lose as moved by you.
We are the flags embroidered with the lion:
The unseen wind which ripples us is you.

Written by Rumi, his *Mathnawi* was held by Jami to be the
Qur'an rendered into Persian – in other words, to be the
nearest to the manifestation of God that is possible in this
world. For Rumi, as indeed for the Prophet Muhammad
before him, everything is subordinate to the absolute unity
of God: if there *is* God, then there can only be what God is.
Every aspect of life, including the beauties of the world,
must necessarily be derived from God's creative act.
Humans have the power to discern this, so that their
greatest freedom is to acknowledge, with soul-burning
marvel, the generosity of God. The Qur'an says, 'We have
honoured the children of Adam' (s.xvii.70). Rumi commented
on that verse: 'People are mounted on the horseback of the
word, "We have honoured the children of Adam": the reins
of freewill are in the hands of their discernment.' It is
possible, therefore, to use one's freewill in such a way that
one follows the satans down to the 'lowest of the low'
(s.xcv.5). The antidote to that disaster is not sentiment but
seeing – seeing everything in this world, not as the only
reality with which we have to deal, but as a shadow thrown
into our midst from the Source of its appearance:

Dipping on high the bird, the shadow, bird-like, below:
The fool hunts the shadow, racing till he sinks exhausted,
Not knowing that it is but a trace of the bird in the sky,
    not knowing the Source of the shadow.

The quest for a union with the Source of the shadows in
this world led undoubtedly to ecstatic poetry of love of
immense beauty. But it led also to anxiety and trouble,
because it seemed that such poets were claiming in their
union of love with God to have become identical with God.
The eye neither rests upon the surface of the glass, nor
even looks through it into some deeper truth, but realises a

union amounting virtually to identity with the very glass on which it looks. It is this which makes sense of the otherwise complex imagery of Attar's *Parliament of Birds*, when the birds attain the object of their quest and find it to be not other than themselves:

Once more they ventured from the dust to raise
Their eyes – up to the Throne – into the blaze,
And in the centre of the glory there
Behold the figure of – *Themselves* – as 'twere
Transfigured – looking to Themselves, beheld
The Figure on the Throne en-miracled,
Until their eyes themselves and *That* between
Did hesitate which *Seer* was, which *Seen*;
They That, That They; Another, yet the Same;
Di-vidual, yet One: from whom there came
A voice of awful answer, scarce discern'd,
From *which* to Aspiration *whose* return'd
They scarcely knew; as when some man apart
Answers aloud the question in his heart:
'The Sun of my perfection is a glass
Wherein from seeing into Being pass
All who, reflecting, as reflected see
Themselves in Me, and Me in them; not *Me*,
But all of me that a contracted eye
Is comprehensive of Infinity;
Nor yet *Themselves*: no selves, but of the All
Fractions, from which they split and whither fall,
As water lifted from the deep, again
Falls back in individual drops of rain,
Then melts into the universal main.
Not all you have been, and seen, and done, and thought,
Not *You* but *I*, have seen and been and wrought:
I was the sin that from Myself rebell'd;
I the remorse that tow'rd Myself compell'd;
I was the Tajidar who led the track;
I was the little briar that pull'd you back:
Sin and contrition – retribution owed,
And cancell'd – pilgrim, pilgrimage, and road,
Was but Myself toward Myself; and Your

Arrival but *Myself* at my own door;
Who in your fraction of Myself behold
Myself within the mirror Myself hold
To see Myself in, and each part of Me
That sees himself, though drown'd, shall ever see.
Come you lost atoms, to your centre Draw,
And *be* the Eternal Mirror that you saw:
Rays that have wander'd into darkness wide
Return, and back into your Sun subside.'

It was this finding of God everywhere in the places of his
creation that led to so many extreme statements by Sufis of
their union with God – and none more so, it seemed, than
those of al-Hallaj:

I am he whom I love, and he whom I love is I.
We are two spirits dwelling in one body.
When you see me, you see him.
When you see him, you see us.

It was al-Hallaj who uttered the famous phrase which led,
indirectly, to his execution, *ana 'lHaqq*, I am the Real. But
since alHaqq – what Hopkins was later, in another tradition, to call 'Ground of being, and granite of it' – is one
of the ninety-nine Beautiful names of God, it seemed
obvious that al-Hallaj was claiming to be God. He was in
fact tried and condemned for the offence of claiming that
one can make a spiritual substitute for the Pilgrimage to
Mecca (one of the indispensable Pillars of Islam); yet it was
his more general teaching which caused alarm; and for that
he was brutally executed in Baghdad, saying 'Do with me
what you will: all who have known ecstasy long for this,
alone at last with the Alone.'

Ana 'l-Haqq: yet in fact that fatal phrase needs to be read in
context: 'If you do not recognise God, at least recognise his
signs. I am that sign, I am the Real, because through the
Real I am made real for ever.' And there we are, back with
the controlling theme of Muslim poetry, that since all
things and all places are a consequence of God's creative act,
all, when they are unblemished, point as signs toward God –
above all, when, as in the human case, that union with God

is deliberately sought and realized. As al-Hallaj put it in one of his poems (using the phrase, according to most texts, *ana haqq*, 'I am *a* reality'):

> Unite me to yourself, you who are one to me,
> By my true stating of your unity,
> For to this unity, no human path can go.
> I am a reality, and this I know,
> Because the Real makes a reality to be
> When with his essence he envelops me.
> No separation then, his radiant light
> Illuminates all things and makes them bright.

al-Hallaj, therefore, was seeking, not a union of total identity (as the Sufi claim of *wahdat al-wujud* might be interpreted), but a unity of self-evident witness, *wahdat al-shuhud*: his life, and every human life, should glow with God. Supremely, the Prophet Muhammad is the Perfect Man, *alLnsan alKamil*, in whom the divine light shines, the visible manifestation of God: 'He is the mirror by which God is revealed to himself.' But even then, the created things and places of the world will also remain as signs, pointing beyond themselves to that union with God from whose hand, as their Creator, they come. Here is the ground of trust, even when God seems absent from the soul:

> O seven seas, bestrew pearls and transmute these things
>   of brass;
> O candle of drunkards and cypress of the garden,
>   how long these tricks? At least keep faith.
> Every granite rock wept for us, Beloved;
>   cure this our pain.
> You angrily turned away your face; for a moment have
>   done with this behaviour.
> You once showed much beneficence and humanity;
>   redouble that humanity.
> Fair of course, O moon and star, be generous in the
>   darkness of night like the moon.
> Separate from us the ancient pain, the anguish of
>   sickness, and the orphan's dust.

Though I be in paradise, in gold and silver,
   without you I am an orphan; cure me.
I have closed my lips and sat in sorrow;
   open my hand, make for encounter.

SIX

❄ *Tagore and India*

On June 5th, 1916, Rabindranath Tagore arrived by train at Tokyo Central station, to be greeted by a vast and enthusiastic crowd of at least 20,000 people. The spiritual ambassador of India, he had been awarded the Nobel prize for literature only three years before – the West acknowledging the East. Yet Tagore was deeply protestant against the West, which in his view had lost its soul in the embattled pursuit of material gain. On the last day of the old century, he had written:

> The last sun of the century sets amidst the blood-red
>   clouds of the West and the whirlwind of hatred.
> The naked passion of self-love of Nations, in its drunken
>   delirium of greed, is dancing to the clash of steel
>   and the howling verses of vengeance.
>
> The hungry self of the Nation shall burst in a violence
>   of fury from its own shameless feeding.
> For it has made the world its food.
> And licking it, crunching it, and swallowing it in big
>   morsels,
> It swells and swells,
> Till in the midst of its unholy feast descends the sudden
>   shaft of heaven piercing its heart of grossness.

But from where will this light dawn? Only, Tagore thought, from the East: 'Who knows', he said, in one of his speeches in Japan, 'if that day has not already dawned, and the sun not risen in the easternmost horizon of Asia? And I offer, as did my ancestor *rsis*, my salutation to that sunrise of the east, which is destined once again to illumine the whole world.' The East for him was the place of a poetry which would heal the world of its madness. When he visited the Zen Sojiji near Yokohama, he referred to the place of pilgrimage in India where the Ganges and the Jumna flow together, and then he said: 'My journey to Japan is like the journey of a pilgrim to a sacred place.'

Yet in fact 'the spiritual East', supposedly superior to the materialism of the West, was itself a largely Western construction: it was put together by nineteenth-century Transcendentalists or by besieged Romantics – like Matthew Arnold, who wrote of the Roman conquest of Palestine:

> The East bow'd low before the blast
> In patient, deep disdain;
> She let the legions thunder past,
> And plunged in thought again.

Ex oriente lux, out of the East, light – that light of the rising sun which, on one occasion early in his life, had delivered to Tagore an unforgettable experience of absolute beauty and truth. But, in Japan, 'the Rising Sun' had entirely different connotations and ambitions; and Tagore's lectures and visit ended in rejection and fiasco. The perceptive C. F. Andrews observed:

> They received him with enthusiasm at first, as one who had brought honour to Asia. But when he spoke out strongly against the militant imperialism which he saw on every side in Japan and set forward in contrast his ideal picture of the true meeting of East and West, with its vista of world brotherhood, the hint went abroad that such 'pacifist' teaching was a danger in war-time, and that the Indian poet represented a defeated nation. Therefore, almost as rapidly as the enthusiasm had arisen, it subsided. In the end, he was almost isolated, and the object for which he had come to the Far East remained unfulfilled.

But eight years later, he made a second attempt to realize the dream, this time in China. He arrived on April 23rd, 1924, at Chi'en Men station in Peking, to the greeting of exploding firecrackers but a much smaller crowd. Again he made the claim that he was coming to China in homage:

I have come to China, not with the attitude of a tourist . . . or as a missionary bringing a gospel, but only as one seeking wisdom, like a pilgrim wishing to pay homage to the ancient culture of China, in an attitude of reverence and love.

Almost his last poem (dictated, because he was too weak to write) recalled the experience of human unity and identity which he encountered in China, and which echoed his own experience of the unity of the universe from which all other unities derive:

Once I went to the land of China.
Those whom I had not met
Put the mark of friendship on my forehead,
Calling me their own.

The garb of a stranger slipped from me unknowing.
The inner man appeared who is eternal,
Revealing a joyous relationship, unforeseen.

A Chinese name I took, dressed in Chinese clothes.
This I know in my mind:
Wherever I find my friend, there I am born anew.

Yet for all that, the result of his visit was the same: what has China to do with India? Tagore was angrily rejected, not least for the very reverence which he showed for the ancient culture:

We have had enough of the ancient Chinese civilisation, which crushed the people and enriched the prince, which subjected women and exalted men, which produced feudal fiefs supporting an aristocracy. We have suffered enough from these things! We want no more of them! But Mr. Tagore wants to take us back to the civilisation of those bygone ages. Therefore we must protest against him.

In the face of these protests, Tagore cancelled the last three of his lectures and left China assailed by shouts and placards, 'We don't want philosophy, we want materialism!' He returned to India, believing that *this* was the place which would have to awaken the world, including the rest of Asia, 'to the heaven of freedom . . . where words come out from the depth of truth'. In this return to India, there was at least emotional sense. To the brahmans, India had always been the place of civilization, beyond whose borders to the north lay nothing but disorder. To leave India was to lose one's status as a brahman. In the great epic, the *Mahabharata*, there is a pilgrimage section, *Tirtha-yatra*, which describes the route whereby the whole of India becomes a place of pilgrimage. So the place of poetry, through which alone the world can be halted in its rush to self-destruction, cannot be other than Bharat, India:

> On the shores of Bharat,
> Where men of all races have come together,
> Awake, O my mind!
> I send my salutations to the God of humanity,
> And in solemn chant sing his praises.
> At whose call no one knows
> Came floating streams of men
> And merged into the sea of Bharat.
> The Aryan, the non-Aryan, the Dravidian,
> The Huns, the Pathans and the Moghuls –
> They all have merged here into one body.
> Today the West has opened its doors,
> And from thence come gifts.
> Giving and taking,
> All will be welcome on the shores of Bharat,
> Where men of all races have come together.
>
> Come, O Aryan and non-Aryan,
> Hindu and Muslim,
> Come, O English and you Christian,
> Come, O Brahmin,
> Purify your mind and clasp the hand of all;
> Come, O downtrodden,
> And let vanish all burdens of your humiliation.
> Tarry not, but come you all
> To anoint the Mother,
> On the shores of Bharat,
> Where men of all races have come together.

But that rather dull recital hardly catches the ethos of the land, still less the poetry of its places. For Tagore, that poetry derived from his single moment of experience when he watched the sun rise one morning and felt a complete unity and harmony in the entire universe – and his own identity with it:

> A sudden spring breeze of religious experience for the first time came to my life and passed away, leaving in my memory a direct message of spiritual reality. . . . This experience seemed to tell me of the stream of melody issuing from the very heart of the universe and spreading over space and time, re-echoing thence as waves of joy which flow right back to the source.

As with Traherne (pp. 14f), this experience transfigured for Tagore the entire universe of his encounter, so that it no longer seemed to be 'like heaps of things and happenings', and even people passing in the street 'seemed to me all so extraordinarily wonderful as they flowed past – waves on the sea of the universe'. From that experience, the unities of time and space become unequivocal:

> What does the old man hope for from those books
> like graves
> When the whole earth is his carpet,
> And the stars are a rosary within his hands?

The consequence can be seen when Tagore turned his gaze to what is perhaps the best known place in the whole of India – at least to the outsider: the Taj-Mahal.

> This you knew, O Emperor Shahjahan,
> That youth, glory and riches all pass away
> In the stream of Time.
> 'Might the sorrow of his heart
> Be made deathless',
> That was the desire of the Emperor.
> Let the pomp of regal power
> Vanish like the last glow of the sunset sky,
> But may one deep sigh
> Make tender the heavens,

This was your wish.
The lustre of all your diamonds and pearls
Is like the rainbow,
Spreading enchantment over the distant sky;
If that lustre dims, let it vanish,
But may this Taj-Mahal glisten bright
Like a tear drop on the cheek of Time.
Oh mind of Man,
You have no time to look backwards,
You hurry along the stream of life from port to port,
Taking up burdens at one
And laying them down at the other.
At the whisper of the south wind,
The spring flowers at the skirt of the forest,
Are scattered to dust,
At the approach of twilight.
There is no time to linger.
Therefore in the wintry night the Kunda
Blossoms anew to adorn tearful autumn's tray of delight.
O Heart, you must leave all your gatherings by the
    wayside,
At the end of the day,
At the end of the night,
There is no time to linger and look backward.
And so, Emperor, your anxious heart
Had desired to steal the heart of Time
Through Beauty's enchantment.
Flinging that garland round her neck,
You have given to death that is formless,
A form immortal.
There is no time to mourn in the busy flow of the years,
Therefore you have prisoned your restless cry
In the silent net of stern marble.
The love-names you used to call your beloved
On moon-lit nights in the privacy of your chamber,
Those whispering love-calls you have here left behind
In the ear of the Infinite.
The tearful tenderness of love has blossomed
In these quiet stones as the flowers of Beauty.
O Poet-Emperor, this dream-picture of your heart,

This new 'Cloud-Messenger',
Is soaring in songs and rhythms toward that Unseen,
Where your beloved has become one
With the glow of early dawn,
The tender sigh of the weary eventide,
The ethereal loveliness of the Chameli in the moonlight,
And the shoreless region beyond all words
Whence the hungering eye returns baffled
From its quest.
Your messenger of Beauty,
Eluding the watchman of Time,
Proclaims eternally: 'I have not forgotten,
I have not forgotten, O beloved.'

You have passed away, O Emperor.
Your empire has vanished like a dream
And your throne lies in the dust.
The memory of your warriors
Under whose tramp the earth once shuddered,
Is borne on the dust-laden winds of Delhi.
Your musicians sing no more,
The strains of the *nahabat* mingle no more
With the ripples of the Jumna.
The jingling music of the princesses' anklets
Which died down amid the forsaken ruins,
Reappears in the cry of the crickets
And resounds in the darkness of the night.
Still your messenger, untired and unfailing,
Ignoring the rise and fall of empires,
The rhythm of life and death,
Proclaims through the ages
With the voice of the eternal-bereaved:
'I have not forgotten, I have not forgotten,
O beloved.' . . .

Who gives you life, O Stone?
Who provides you,
Year by year, with the nectar of Immortality?
You hold up to the heavens eternally
This Joy-flower of earth,
And round you blows all the year

The sad breath of parting Spring.
The tear-dipped songs that died away
At the end of the night of union,
Lit by the dim candle, are still echoing
Ceaselessly in your heart,
O Stone, deathless Stone!

From his torn heart,
The bereaved Emperor brought out the jewel of separation
And laid it in the hand of the Universe,
For all to behold.
The royal guards are not there to keep watch;
All the heavens embrace her;
The sky imprints on her gently
One silent kiss of Eternity.
The first rays of the morning sun
Throw their crimson glow upon her,
And the pale rays of the moon,
With a sad smile of parting,
Make her tender!

O Empress! through Beauty's enchantment
The memory of your love has become sublime.
That memory, incorporeal and ethereal,
Taking form,
Merges the Emperor's love with the Love universal,
And spreads beyond you to the whole world
In the imperishable light of life!
From the secrecy of the royal chamber
You have brought your glorious crown
And placed it on the heads of all lovers,
From dwellers in palaces to those in the meanest huts.
The memory of your love has sanctified them all.

The Emperor has taken leave of his own royal deed.
Today, the eternal sorrow of the mind of Man,
Embracing this marble Beauty,
Is seeking its realisation night and morn!

With this love of India, it is not surprising that Tagore
wrote the music and words of *Jana Gana Mana*, which, after
Independence, became the national anthem of India:

Thou art the ruler of the minds of all people,
    Thou dispenser of India's destiny.
Thy name arouses the hearts
    Of the Punjab, Sind, Gujrat, and Maratha,
    Of Dravid, Orissa and Bengal.
It echoes in the hills of the Vindhyas and Himalayas,
    Mingles in the music of Jumna and Ganges,
    And is chanted by the waves of the Indian sea.
They pray for thy blessing and sing thy praise,
    Thou dispenser of India's destiny,
Victory, victory, victory to thee.

So Tagore undoubtedly cast the place of poetry too wide when he dreamed of the whole of Asia setting an example of peace to a blood-drunken world of mutual hatreds and greed. But what now of his dream that at least in India the reconciliation of different peoples and different religions can be achieved? At Independence the example was clear to see; what poem would Tagore write now of the place of India as the spiritual conscience of the world? Or would his poetry still remain a prayer?

Where the mind is without fear and the head is held high;
Where knowledge is free;
Where the world has not been broken up into fragments
    by narrow domestic walls;
Where words come out from the depth of truth;
Where tireless striving stretches its arms towards
    perfection;
Where the clear stream of reason has not lost its way
    into the dreary desert sand of dead habit;
Where the mind is led forward by Thee into
    ever-widening thought and action –
Into that heaven of freedom, my Father, let my
    country awake.

SEVEN

❧ American Indians and Africa

It is one thing to allow places of beauty to become the occasion of poetry. But what about places which seem at first sight – at least to *some* people – to be places of ugliness? We can sing with ease of 'all things bright and beautiful':

> The purple-headed mountain,
>   The river running by,
> The sunset in the morning,
>   That brightens up the sky.

But what of Monty Python's alternative version?

> All things dull and ugly
>   All creatures short and squat
> All things rude and nasty
>   The Lord God made the lot.

> Each little snake that poisons
>   Each little wasp that stings
> He made their brutish venom
>   He made their horrid wings.

> All things sick and cancerous
>   All evil great and small
> All things foul and dangerous
>   The Lord God made them all.

> Each little nasty hornet
>   Each beastly little squid
> Who made the spiky urchin,
>   Who made the sharks? He did.

> All things scabbed and ulcerous
>   All pox both great and small
> Putrid, foul and gangrenous,
>   The Lord God made them all.

To which the religious poetry of place, and especially that of the Hindu, replies, 'Of course: how could it possibly be otherwise?' Part of the purpose of Tantra is to help us to look on all manifestation, particularly the foul and gangrenous, as equally the bearer of Brahman, the universal soul, which is always present, in any of the forms it takes:

> I am the taste in the waters,
> I am the light in the moon and the sun . . .
> I am the smell of the earth,
> I am the heat of the fire . . .
> Whatever the forms of being may be
> Peaceful or passionate or heavy with sloth,
> All are from me alone:
> I am not in them; they are in me. (vii.8,9,12)

So Krishna claims in the Song of the Lord, the Bhagavadgita, the most precious poem to virtually all Hindus. But this conversion of the dangerous places occurs in poetry in more religions than that. What place could be more threatening than the arid deserts which lie behind the salt flats on the edge of the Pacific in what is now the south west corner of California? The earliest Western explorers (Lumholtz, for example) regarded themselves as lucky indeed to have extracted themselves and their animals alive. Yet here the Papago Indians made the salt pilgrimage the supreme exploration into the conditions of life and death. In the long 'Wise Talks' of the salt pilgrimage, the young man describes to his guardian the desolation of the land, and then the miracle of life restored on his return:

> 'What will you do, my guardian?
> Yonder see,
> The earth which you have spread thus wretched seems.
> The mountains which you placed erect now crumbling stand.
> The trees you planted have no leaves.
> The birds you threw into the air
> Wretchedly flit therein and do not sing.
> The beasts that run upon the earth
> At the tree roots go digging holes

And make no sound.
The wretched people
See nothing fit to eat.' Thus did I say.
There did the entrails within him crack with pity . . .
'Something,' he said, 'I will cause you to see.' . . .
I saw the land did sloping lie.
Before I had gone far the wind did follow and breathe
    upon me.
Then, down at the foot of the east there moved the
    clouds,
And from their breasts the lightning did go roaring.
Though the earth seemed very wide,
Straight across it fell the rain,
And stabbed the north with its drops.
Straight across it fell the rain
And stabbed the south with its drops.
The flood channels, lying side by side,
Seemed many;
But the water from all directions went filling them
    to the brim.
The ditches lying side by side
Seemed many;
But the water along them went bubbling.
The magicians on the nearby mountains
Went rushing out, gathering themselves together.
The storm went on and on:
It reached the foot of the west, it turned and faced about.
It saw the earth spongy with moisture.

Thus beautifully did my desire end;
Thus perchance you will also feel, my kinsman.

But what of that earth 'spongy with moisture'? What of
mud – that 'fifth element', of Napoleon which, as much as
snow, defeated his armies? 'Somme!' wrote a young
German from France: 'The whole history of the world
cannot contain a more ghastly word.' It evoked from
Wilfred Owen the poetry of pity. Yet in Africa, the places of
mud and silt are the places of the poetry of praise and
thanksgiving, for here, in a dry land, are the origins of
life:

From a water-woven land
came creatures of convoluted imagination.
They know where the power lies –
in essences of female and reptile.
From slime, disease, insects,
the sludge of earth and river
come composite formations
as natural as oil.
It is a subterfuge,
the making of articulate spirit
and lucrative heat.

It becomes clear that the nature of a place does not dictate the poetry which arises from it. It is the acculturated experience of places (which may superficially seem comparable) which writes the words in different ways. Thus the Indians of North America have been dispossessed from the land which once allowed particular styles and ways of life. It is now virtually ritual alone which, when it is enacted, can raise the Lazarus of those lost places from the grave. For that reason, as Jerome Rothenberg's *Shaking the Pumpkin* makes clear, much of their poetry remains strongly connected to ritual:

now the thinkers our old ones remember
    the gods known as dancers

let's call the dancers
talking and thinking
        call them to come
    from their far away sky place
call for the rain gods
        explain the problem

the dancers receive the message
they put on their garments their crowns
their life-giving feathers
black as night
        white as cloud

veil their faces with beads
    talking
their faces are radiant

they take the great cross the great rattle
far away in their sky place
they concentrate
on the high east

then they rise high in the east
radiant as life in their feathers
they come down to talk to the earth

see the life-giving trees
     stand up
line their road

lovely fig trees and tuka trees
lovely anapa trees by their road

lovely the reed
     rising
full of life the banana tree

life-giving reed
        there it stands

then the dancers appear
     down east
stopping to wait for mother and elder brother

'dance you gods
        bring the rain down
dance you dancers
        come down to your earth'
they wait for the fiddles
     for the fiddlers to play
           now they hear them
the sound of their fiddles
     sound known as 'words'

they listen to it
        they start dancing

now it resounds on their earth
   the dance of the 'dancers'
        who call themselves rain gods

and when it is over
they go
talking they go
   west
to see Tsevimoa
the goddess
   who sits on her rainstone
fade in the west with all their thoughts
and the thinkers our old ones
leave them there
in their thought's power
turn back east to the altar
ending
   a good day's work.

That connection of ritual and place is not untrue of Africa. But Africans are returning into possession of their lands, and poets are among the agents of that repossession:

Africa, you were once just a name to me
But now you lie before me with sombre green challenge
To that loud faith for freedom (life more abundant)
Which we once professed shouting
Into the silent listening microphone
Or on an alien platform to a sea
Of white perplexed faces troubled
With secret Imperial guilt; shouting
Of you with a vision euphemistic
As you always appear
To your lonely sons on distant shores.

Then the cold sky and continent would disappear
In a grey mental mist.
And in its stead the hibiscus blooms in shameless scarlet
and the bougainvillea in mauve passion
entwines itself around strong branches
the palm trees stand like tall proud moral women
shaking their plaited locks against the
cool suggestive evening breeze;
the short twilight passes;
the white full moon turns its round gladness

towards the swept open space
between the trees; there will be
dancing tonight; and in my brimming heart
plenty of love and laughter.
Oh, I got tired of the cold northern sun,
Of white anxious ghost-like faces,
Of crouching over heatless fires
In my lonely bedroom.
The only thing I never tired of
was the persistent kindness
Of you too few unafraid
Of my grave dusky strangeness.

So I came back
Sailing down the Guinea Coast.
Loving the sophistication
Of your brave new cities:
Dakar, Accra, Cotonou,
Lagos, Bathurst and Bissau;
Liberia, Freetown, Libreville,
Freedom is really in the mind.

Go up-country, so they said,
To see the real Africa.
For whomsoever you may be,
That is where you come from.
Go for bush, inside the bush,
You will find your hidden heart,
Your mute ancestral spirit.
And so I went, dancing on my way.

Now you lie before me passive
With your unanswering green challenge.
Is this all you are?
This long uneven red road, this occasional succession
Of huddled heaps of four mud walls
And thatched, falling grass roofs
Sometimes ennobled by a thin layer
Of white plaster, and covered with thin
Slanting corrugated zinc.
These patient faces on weather-beaten bodies

Bowing under heavy market loads.
The pedalling cyclist wavers by
On the wrong side of the road,
As if uncertain of his new emancipation.
The squawking chickens, the pregnant she-goats
Lumber awkwardly with fear across the road,
Across the windscreen view of my four-cylinder kit car
An overladen lorry speeds madly towards me
Full of produce, passengers, with driver leaning
Out into the swirling dust to pilot his
Swinging obsessed vehicle along.
Beside him on the raised seat his first-class
Passenger, clutching and timid; but he drives on
At so, so many miles per hour, peering out with
Bloodshot eyes, unshaved face and dedicated look;
His motto painted on each side: *Sunshine Transport,*
We get you there quick, quick. The Lord is my Shepherd.

The red dust settles down on the green leaves.

I know you will not make me want, Lord,
Though I have reddened your green pastures
It is only because I have wanted so much
That I have always been found wanting.
From South and East, and from my West
(The sandy desert holds the North)
We look across a vast continent
And blindly call it ours.
You are not a country, Africa,
You are a concept,
Fashioned in our minds, each to each,
To hide our separate dreams.
Only those within you who know
Their circumscribed plot,
And till it well with steady plough
Can from that harvest then look up
To the vast blue inside
Of the enamelled bowl of sky
Which covers you and say
'This is my Africa' meaning
'I am content and happy.

I am fulfilled, within,
Without and roundabout.
I have gained the little longings
Of my hands, my loins, my heart
And the soul that follows in my shadow.'
I know now that is what you are, Africa:
Happiness, contentment, and fulfilment,
And a small bird singing on a mango tree.

The reality of Africa has not turned out to correspond to the dream: perhaps all visions *are* euphemistic. Even the 'sombre green challenge' seems tragic in the light of so many recurrent droughts and swathes of starvation. Yet still the fact remains that the poetry of place depends for its content and its style on the context in which it occurs; and what is a cause for apprehension in one place is a prompting of praise in another. So it was for an African poet when a man first stepped on the moon:

Gobble the news with seven grains
of alligator pepper, a pinch of salt,
white chalk, one sea-deep cry
for man's hike to Jehovah-hood, or
must we not submerge in rituals
this explosive moment of animal triumph? –
Catch my hand, brother,
we are annexing the kingdom of the gods.

But to walk on the moon while children cannot walk to the next well does not say much for human priorities, or for the moral urgency of scientists who 'do it because it is there'. The poetry of place is not only about places of beauty. And what of places of such evil that they surely negate the nerve of the poet altogether? What of Buchenwald? What of Hiroshima?

EIGHT

✿ Buchenwald
and Hiroshima

It is one thing for a poet to point us to possible virtues in the places of ugliness; it is surely quite another to write poetry in the places of irreversible evil. When evil is spelt 'Buchenwald' or 'Hiroshima', it cannot be converted by a baptism of poetry:

> This is the way in. The words
> Wrought in iron on the gate:
> *Jedem das seine.* Everybody
> Gets what he deserves.
>
> The bare drab rubble of the place.
> The dull damp stone. The rain.
> The emptiness. The human lack.
> *Jedem das seine. Jedem das seine.*
> Everybody gets what he deserves.
>
> It all forms itself
> Into one word: Buchenwald.
> And those who know and those
> Born after that war but living
> In its shadow, shiver at the words.
> Everybody gets what he deserves.
>
> It is so quiet now. So
> Still that it makes an absence.
> At the silence of the metal loads
> We can almost hear again the voices,
> The moaning of the cattle that were men.
> Ahead, acres of abandoned gravel.
> Everybody gets what he deserves.
>
> Wood, beech wood, song
> Of birds. The sky, the usual sky.
> A stretch of trees. A sumptuous sheet

Of colours dragging through the raindrops.
Drizzle loosening the small stones
We stand on. Stone buildings. Doors. Dark.
A dead tree leaning in the rain.
Everybody gets what he deserves.

Cold, numb cold. Despair
And no despair. The very worst
Of men against the very best.
A joy in brutality from lack
Of feeling for the other. The greatest
Evil, racialism. A man, the greatest good.
Much more than a biological beast,
An aggregate of atoms. Much more.
Everybody gets what he deserves.

And it could happen again
And they could hang like broken carcasses
And they could scream in terror without light
And they could count the strokes that split their skin
And they could smoulder under cigarettes
And they could suffer and bear every blow
And they could starve and live for death
And they could live for hope alone
And it could happen again.
Everybody gets what he deserves.

The opening of Alan Bold's 'June 1967 at Buchenwald'. And
Hiroshima? 'The Burden', and 'The Refugee', from Marc
Kaminsky's *The Road From Hiroshima*:

> The Burden
> 1.
> He was the only one
> making his way toward the city
>
> blue-green fire-balls
> drifted around him
>
> dim figures
> moved in the darkness
>
> against the injured sky
> the injured began to appear

2.
He saw

3.
one without eyebrows
then one bald
and vomiting as she walked
then one with black skin

and one with the skin of her back
hanging down
like a sheet of wet newspaper
and one mumbling prayers

and one holding a clock
straight-armed in front of his body
its low clean ticking
uncanny as a gong

and one with the bone
showing through
at the shoulder, cradling
the lifeless arm in the good one

then one leading a child
by the hand, and finding
it wasn't hers
shaking it loose

and one who couldn't be seen
under a burning house
calling, 'Help if you please!'
and a gingko tree

burnt through, carbonized
in the shape of a tree
its great roots thrust out
into the air

and a naked one carrying a corpse
and pleading for water
and one whose disheveled hair
was caked with blood

then an old one half-dragging
a woman whose head
rolled heavily back and forth
then one with a fishing rod

then one who halted, who would not
go on in the black rain
and one with a wheelbarrow
full of papers

and one in white trousers
who crept along
on all fours, noiselessly sobbing
and one whose legs pumped

furiously up and down
who was wedged in
with a group of the dead and dying
who got nowhere

4.
And as he ran
toward the city, lacerated
with shame
that he alone was unhurt

he turned to the left and the right
and he said as he ran
past each of them, 'Excuse me
that I have no burden like yours.'

5.
No one wept
no one screamed in pain
none of the dying
died noisily
not even the children
cried
no one spoke

All day they poured
into the grove by the river
to hide under green
leaves

and all day the unwounded one
brought them water

He could not tell
the living from the dead

he brought water
to the lips of each body
that lay there
and if one drank
that meant his suffering
had not yet ended

Over and over he had to tell himself
'These are human beings'
as he gave the bottle
to those whose faces had been blotted out

and sometimes
after they tried to take in some water
they raised their bodies a little
and bowed to him in thanks.

The Refugee
1.
I waited, my air-raid
hood covering most of the burn
and my head bowed

at the edge of my village I waited
one of the faceless ones

   they closed their gates against us
and turned their eyes
on the road
from Hiroshima I became invisible

then the black market woman came by
I got up and said: Taka Mitsuda
I would be deeply obliged if you would bring me
a mirror

then I went back
into the fields

2.
Can this be my face?

Taking one end of a curled-up piece
of skin
I tugged at it gently

It hurt
which assured me
that the face giving me this wary look
was mine

How can this be? I thought
peeling away each purple-black ridge
a bit at a time
like you play with a loose tooth
hating and enjoying the pain
I stripped off all the dead skin

3.
And then I turned to face them.

But there was also a place called Golgotha, the place of a
skull. There, it is not the unwounded man who offers water
to the afflicted, but the wounded and afflicted man who
drinks the bitterness of gall and vinegar, in unevaded death;
and from that death he not only tells the living from the
dead, but brings, from the dead, the resurrection and the
life:

I am the blown shell, the wasted seed,
I am the fallen sky, the broken reed,
I am expelled from nurture, from the nest,
I have not means to mend – nor strength addressed
To restitution. If sparrows fall
Shall that perfection, broken, hear its call?
Lord, lean from that extended arm,
Be it by nails, alleviate from harm.

In truth, deeply and always in truth, the crucifixion does
not erase or diminish or make less than evil the realities of
evil. Nevertheless, it transmits the signals of redemption
even into those most desolate domains of the devil: London,

1940, the target of terror and of undiscriminating murder by those who were equally responsible for Buchenwald:

Still falls the Rain –
Dark as the world of man, black as our loss –
Blind as the nineteen hundred and forty nails
Upon the Cross.
Still falls the Rain
With a sound like the pulse of the heart that is changed to
   the hammer-beat
In the Potter's Field, and the sound of the impious feet

On the tomb:
               Still falls the rain
In the Field of Blood where the small hopes breed and the
   human brain
Nurtures its greed, that worm with the brow of Cain.

Still falls the Rain –
At the feet of the Starved Man hung upon the Cross.
Christ that each day, each night, nails there, have mercy
   on us –
On Dives and on Lazarus:
Under the Rain the sore and the gold are as one.

Still falls the Rain –
Still falls the blood from the Starved Man's wounded
   Side:
He bears in His Heart all wounds, – those of the light that
   died,
The last faint spark
In the self-murdered heart, the wounds of the sad
   uncomprehending dark,
The wounds of the baited bear, –
The blind and weeping bear whom the keepers beat
On his helpless flesh . . . the tears of the hunted hare.

Still falls the Rain –
Then – O Ile leape up to my God: who pulles me doune –
See, see where Christ's blood streames in the firmament:
It flows from the Brow we nailed upon the tree
Deep to the dying, to the thirsting heart

That holds the fires of the world, – dark-smirched with
   pain
As Caesar's laurel crown.

Then sounds the voice of One who like the heart of man
Was once a child who among beasts has lain –
'Still do I love, still shed my innocent light, my Blood, for
   thee.'

'He descended into hell': at the head of his poem, *The Road from Hiroshima*, Kaminsky set these words from Jonathan Schell:

It may be only by descending into this hell in imagination
now that we can hope to escape descending into it in
reality at some later time. The knowledge we thus gain
cannot in itself protect us from nuclear annihilation, but
without it we cannot begin to take the measures that can
actually protect us.

So Alan Bold concluded his poem on Buchenwald:

We turn away. We always do.
It's what we turn into that matters.
From the invisible barracks of Buchenwald
Where only an unsteady horizon
Remains. The dead cannot complain.
They never do. But we, we live.
Everybody gets what he deserves.

That which once united man
Now drives him apart. We are not helpless
Creatures crashing onwards irresistibly to doom.
There is time for everything and time to choose
For everything. We are that time, that choice.
Everybody gets what he deserves.

This happened near the core
Of a world's culture. This
Occurred among higher things.
This was a philosophical conclusion.
Everybody gets what he deserves.

The bare drab rubble of the place.
The dull damp stone. The rain.
The emptiness. The human lack.

And Marc Kaminsky ended his narrative poem with a section, 'Watchman: from the Journals of Nakajima Hiroshi'. Nakajima recognises the ambivalence of making his subject matter 'the place of a skull'; yet, he feels the obligation of love, like the faithful women who, in that other tradition, waited at the foot of the cross:

> As I step off the platform
> after reciting my poems
>
> I am abashed
>
> I feel more frail than ever
>
> facing
> the tears and gratitude that I evoke
> and my immense hunger
> for both
>
> suddenly
> I can't tell
> the difference between being
> a profiteer
> on the spiritual black market
>
> and a prophet
> who must tear everyone's heart
> to shreds
>
> as I wrote
> I felt possessed by the dead calling
> for peace
>
> Now I wonder –
>
> is it so laudable
> to spend my days summoning
> images of nuclear war?
>
> yet how
> can I give up
> this fire
> without betraying
> myself and all that
> I love

NINE

✿ The City

Our Father, who art in heaven,
Stay there,
And we will stay here on earth,
Which is at times so lovely
With its mysteries of New York
With its mysteries of Paris
Which absolutely outweigh the mystery of the Trinity.

But who says that the Trinity is not present in the city?
If the Trinity is communication, relationship and love – if,
that is, the human imagination, whether Hindu or Christian,
could not seriously conceive of God as not bearing within
her/his own nature the necessary good of creative interaction
– then the city is the nearest image of God that can be found
on this earth:

Earth has not anything to show more fair:
Dull would he be of soul who could pass by
A sight so touching in its majesty:
This City now doth, like a garment, wear
The beauty of the morning; silent, bare,
Ships, towers, domes, theatres, and temples lie
Open unto the fields, and to the sky;
All bright and glittering in the smokeless air.
Never did sun more beautifully steep
In his first splendour, valley, rock, or hill;
Ne'er saw I, never felt, a calm so deep!
The river glideth at his own sweet will:
Dear God! the very houses seem asleep;
And all that mighty heart is lying still!

This was the very poem which Wallace Stevens chose to
illustrate his claim that the poet's task is to create 'the
supreme fictions'. The role of the poet, according to Stevens,
is 'to help people live their lives'.

If we go back to the collection of solid, static objects extended in space, which Dr. Joad [scientifically] posited, and if we say that the space is blank space, nowhere, without colour, and that the objects, though solid, have no shadows and, though static, exert a mournful power, and, without elaborating this complete poverty, if suddenly we hear a different and familiar description of the place:

This city now doth, like a garment, wear
The beauty of the morning . . .

if we have this experience, we know how poets help people to live their lives. This illustration must serve for all the rest. There is, in fact, a world of poetry indistinguishable from the world in which we live, or, I ought to say, no doubt, from the world in which we shall come to live, since what makes the poet the potent figure that he is, or was, or ought to be, is that he creates the world to which we turn incessantly and without knowing it, and that he gives to life the supreme fictions without which we are unable to conceive of it.

A scientist can hope to describe the cosmos somewhat as it might be even if she were not here to describe it – 'somewhat', because her measurements will distrurb what she observes. But the poet creates the worlds, the places, as we live them:

There was such beauty in the dappled valley
As hurt the sight, as stabbed the heart to tears.
The gathered loveliness of all the years
Hovered thereover, it seemed, eternally
Set for men's joy. Town, tower, trees, river
Under a royal azure sky for ever
Up-piled with snowy towering bulks of cloud:
A herald day of spring more wonderful
Then her true own. Trumpets cried aloud
In sky, earth, blood; no beast, no clod so dull
But the power felt of the day, and of the giver
Was glad for life, humble at once and proud.
Kyrie Eleison, and Gloria,
Credo, Jubilate, Magnificat:
The whole world gathered strength to praise the day.

The city is an ambiguous place, but it is not incapable of glory, for those who have eyes to see:

> Bear in mind, o ye recording angels,
> That all of us, from the Pope to Stalin,
> From Lavatory Dan to John D.Rockefeller,
> Are children gazing in a sweetshop window.

But what of that other image of the city, the City of Destruction, the City of Dreadful Night? 'God the first garden made, and the first city, Cain.'

> He came to the desert of London town
>   Grey miles long;
> He wander'd up and he wander'd down,
>   Singing a quiet song.
>
> He came to the desert of London town,
>   Mirk miles broad;
> He wander'd up and he wander'd down,
>   Ever alone with God.
>
> There were thousands and thousands of human kind
>   In this desert of brick and stone:
> But some were deaf and some were blind,
>   And he was there alone.
>
> At length the good hour came; he died
>   As he had lived, alone:
> He was not miss'd from the desert wide, –
>   Perhaps he was found at the Throne.

So yes, dead would he be of soul who could pass by the wounds – and the wounded – of the city. The wounded traveller, whom most pass by, is safely removed from us on a country road, half-way between Jericho and Jerusalem; but the victim now of the mugging or the rape or the inequalities which build cardboard cities everywhere from New York to Calcutta is not on a country road discreetly distanced from us in a parable: she is here on the sidewalk of the city. For many, therefore, 'Inglan is a Bitch', and London with it:

w'en mi jus' come to Landan toun
mi use to work pan di andahgroun
but workin' pan di andahgroun
y'u don't get fi know your way aroun'

Inglan is a bitch
dere's no escapin' it
Inglan is a bitch
dere's no runnin' whey fram it

mi get a lickle jab in a big 'otell
an' awftah a while, mi woz doin' quite well
dem staat mi aaf as a dish-washah
but w'en mi tek a stack, mi noh tun clack-watchah!

Inglan is a bitch
dere's no escapin' it
Inglan is a bitch
noh baddah try fi hide fram it

w'en dem gi' you di lickle wage packit
fus dem rab it wid dem big tax rackit
y'u haffi struggle fi mek en's meet
an' w'en y'u goh a y'u bed y'u jus' cant sleep

Inglan is a bitch
dere's no escapin' it
Inglan is a bitch fi true
a noh lie mi a tell, a true

mi use to work dig ditch w'en it cowl noh bitch
mi did strang like a mule, but, bwoy, mi did fool
den awftah a while mi jus' stap dhu ovahtime
den awftah a while mi jus' phu dung mi tool

Inglan is a bitch
dere's no escapin' it
Inglan is a bitch
y'u haffi know how fi suvvive in it

well mi dhu day wok an' mi dhu nite wok
mi dhu clean wok an' mi dhu dutty wok
dem seh dat black man is very lazy
but if y'u si how mi wok y'u woulda sey mi crazy

Inglan is a bitch
dere's no escapin' it
Inglan is a bitch
y'u bettah face up to it

dem have a lickle facktri up inna a Brackly
inna disya facktri all dem dhu is pack crackry
fi di laas fifteen years dem get mi laybah
now awftah fifteen years mi fall out a fayvah

Inglan is a bitch
dere's no escapin' it
Inglan is a bitch
dere's no runnin' whey fram it

mi know dem have work, work in abundant
yet still, dem mek mi redundant
now, at fifty-five mi gettin' quite ol'
yet still, dem sen' mi fi goh draw dole

Inglan is a bitch
dere's no escapin' it
Inglan is a bitch fi true
is whey wi a goh dhu 'bout it?

Cities as we live them always challenge us with that
question, with the mysteries of good and evil within them,
as Thomas Rock perceived:

How strange and beautiful the city looks today. A city
where good men walk in dignity and peace, and children
play in green places, and girls are both pure and merry,
and the hearts of young men are lifted with the
aspirations of love, and scholars labour diligently with no
other motive than the advancement of knowledge and
happiness of mankind. Dear me! Who would think that
that lovely city below us is a Gibraltar of propriety and
mediocrity, where the good men starve or are hounded
into the dark, and the worthless thrive, and the scholars
think only of material rewards, and the girls are born
with their noses snobbed in the air and their eyes
searching for a marriage bargain, and the young men's
hearts are lifted only by the thought of easy success. And

who would think, too, that within that Gibraltar lies an *inner* island of active evil.

With that recognition, and in those circumstances, the poetry of place in the city can rightly become prophetic, calling us to the rescue of relationship, and of that lost majesty which Wordsworth saw; for the man of whom James Thomson wrote (p. 64) in 'the desert of London town', was William Blake:

> 'Do I sleep amidst danger to my friends? O my Cities and Counties,
> Do you sleep? rouze up, rouze up! Eternal death is abroad!'
> So Albion spoke, and threw himself into the furnaces of affliction.

If we hear that call, then the poetry of the city will still supply the images of our own renewal. Jerusalem can be exactly that controlling metaphor, as it was for Blake (p. *ix*); Byzantium can still remain, as it was for Yeats, the architecture of our own intent:

> That is no country for old men. The young
> In one another's arms; birds in the trees,
> – Those dying generations – at their song;
> The salmon-falls, the mackerel-crowded seas,
> Fish, flesh, or fowl, commend all summer long
> Whatever is begotten, born, and dies.
> Caught in that sensual music all neglect
> Monuments of unageing intellect.
>
> An aged man is but a paltry thing,
> A tattered coat upon a stick, unless
> Soul clap its hands and sing, and louder sing
> For every tatter in its mortal dress,
> Nor is there singing school but studying
> Monuments of its own magnificence;
> And therefore I have sailed the seas and come
> To the holy city of Byzantium.
>
> O sages standing in God's holy fire
> As in the gold mosaic of a wall,

Come from the holy fire, perne in a gyre,
And be the singing-masters of my soul.
Consume my heart away; sick with desire
And fastened to a dying animal
It knows not what it is; and gather me
Into the artifice of eternity.

Once out of nature I shall never take
My bodily form from any natural thing,
But such a form as Grecian goldsmiths make
Of hammered gold and gold enamelling
To keep a drowsy Emperor awake;
Or set upon a golden bough to sing
To lords and ladies of Byzantium
Of what is past, or passing, or to come.

TEN

❧ *Jerusalem*

The poetry of the city may be a poetry of protest, but it can also be a poetry of peace – as it was for Wordsworth: 'Ne'er saw I, never felt a calm so deep.' But translated into another language, the place of peace is Jerusalem. *Urushalem* meant originally 'foundation of the god Shalem', an Ugaritic Canaanite god, who had made Jerusalem a sacred city long before David captured it – 'Even the blind and the lame will stop you coming in here' (2 Sam. 5.6); but by a play on words, the sacred city, when it *was* captured, was converted into the city of God's messianic peace, into Zion; and it became the great place of Hebrew poetry, of both literal and metaphorical pilgrimage:

> I was glad when they said to me: let us go to the house of the Lord.
> And now our feet are standing: within your gates, O Jerusalem –
> Jerusalem which is built as a city: where the pilgrims gather in unity.
> There the tribes go up, the tribes of the Lord:
>   as he commanded Israel to give thanks to the name of the Lord.
> There are set thrones of judgement: the thrones of the house of David.
> O pray for the peace of Jerusalem: may those who love you prosper.
> Peace be within your walls: prosperity in your palaces.
> For the sake of my brothers and companions: I will pray that peace be with you.
> For the sake of the house of the Lord our God: I will seek for your good.

The Psalms become the most familiar of all the poetries of place and praise. Even when Jerusalem fell to the Babylonians, and most of its inhabitants were taken into exile, Jerusalem remained the centre of their world:

> By the waters of Babylon we sat down and wept:
>> when we remembered Zion.
> We took our harps and hung them up:
>> on the trees that are in that land.
> For there, our captors demanded a song:
>> and those who had destroyed us demanded mirth:
>> 'Sing us,' they said, 'one of the songs of Zion.'
> How can we sing the Lord's song:
>> in a strange land?
> If I forget you, O Jerusalem:
>> may my right hand lose its cunning!
> May my tongue stick to the roof of my mouth:
>> if I do not keep you in mind, if I do not count
>> Jerusalem my greatest joy!

When the Exile ended and the Jews were restored to Jerusalem, it seemed as though the guarantee of God to Zion had indeed been fulfilled; and the Jewish imagination endowed Jerusalem with almost supernatural qualities: Jerusalem is the centre of the world, the mother of all nations, whose beauties exceed all other beauties in the world. Here all the great events of history took place, from creation (the *eben shetiyyah*, the foundation stone of the world, can still be seen in Jerusalem), through the Aqedah (the Binding) of Isaac on Mount Moriah (identified with Jerusalem) to the establishing of the Holy of Holies in the Temple. Even the greatest events in the future, the final Day and the resurrection of the dead, will take place in Jerusalem. But that devotion to Jerusalem did not exempt it from further catastrophe: when the Romans captured Jerusalem for a second time, in 135 CE, the site of the Temple was razed and ploughed with salt, and the Jews began their much longer exile, bound to Christian and gentile altars of a more completed death. So began the longing of a return of the scattered exiles to Jerusalem:

> My heart is in the East,
> And I am at the edge of the West.

So how can I taste what I eat,
Or how delight in it?
How can I fulfill my vow to return
While Zion is in the hand of Edom,
And I am in the bond of Arabia?
Better would it be for me to shed the good things of
  Spain,
Glorious for my eyes to see the dust of the ruined shrine.

So wrote Judah haLevi, perhaps the greatest, certainly the most influential, of the medieval Jewish poets. His dream of a return to Zion, at least for himself, came very close to fulfillment: his experience of Christian and Muslim hostility against the Jews in Spain led him, through great dangers, to Egypt. But there, so close to his dream, he died. According to legend, he got even closer to Jerusalem. It is said that he actually completed that final journey, composing and reciting his famous 'Songs of Zion'. According to tradition, he was trampled to death by Muslim horsemen at the gates of Jerusalem while reciting this poem:

O Zion, will you not ask me
About the well-being of your captives,
Those who seek after your peace,
And those who are the remnant of your flock?
From west and east, from north and south,
From every side, accept the greeting of peace;
And 'Peace!' from this captive of desire,
Who sheds his tears like the dew of Hermon,
And longs for them to fall on your hills.
I am like a jackal when I howl for your affliction,
But when I dream of the return of your exiles
I am a lute for your songs.

Out of the depth of that feeling, the strong impetus of Zionism won the argument for Jerusalem in the nineteenth century. The quest for a Jewish homeland had looked for a politically feasible solution: perhaps it should be established in Argentina, or Uganda, or el Arish? Even Theodore Herzl, whose brief essay, *Der Judenstaat*, has been regarded as 'the beginning of modern political Zionism', left it open whether the Jewish state should be in Palestine or Argentina: 'Shall we choose Palestine or Argentina? We shall take what is given us, and what is selected by Jewish public opinion.'

As that opinion formed, it became obvious that any settlements outside Palestine would only be regarded as staging-posts on the way back to Jerusalem. At the Sixth Zionist Congress, furious arguments broke out between those who wanted settlements and those who wanted only Jerusalem. Herzl tried, despairingly, to reconcile them and to save the Zionist movement. At one point, he withdrew from the conference hall, and virtually broke down. But then he recovered himself, and returned for a final and decisive speech: raising his right hand high in the air, he cried out, 'If I forget you, O Jerusalem, may my right hand lose its cunning!' It was one of the supreme moments when the poetry of place has moved the political configurations of the world beyond prediction: from that time on, there was no serious challenge to Jerusalem as the goal.

But the seeds of conflict were equally and unavoidably sown as well; for that same Psalm ends with verses of revenge:

O daughter of Babylon, you that lay waste:
    happy shall he be who serves you as you have served
    us;
Happy shall he be who takes your little ones:
    and dashes them against the stone.

Many Christians now excise those verses when they recite them in church. But the Jewish people have, more often, excised those verses from the practice of their lives. They have not slaughtered the innocents, as Christians all too frequently have done. The challenge, now, of the peace which belongs to Jerusalem is whether, in relation to the Palestinians, it *requires* the implementing of those final verses. Jews know only too well what it is to be on the receiving end of the *un*peaceful, and yet somehow, by the grace of their vocation, they have been able to see the things that belong more truly to their peace. As I wrote in the book, *A Year to Live*:

Among the many images from that Europe which burn themselves as with acid into the mind is a photograph which shows a father leading his child to death in a gas chamber. The boy looks up at his father, who is pointing to heaven. There have been critics who have asked, 'Why did he not resist? Why did he not rush against the rifles with bare hands, rather than die so meekly?' And to that a rabbi once answered, 'Because he had more important things to do.' He had to comfort his son in his last moments of his existence on this earth, surrounding him by love and distancing them both together from that violence outside and all around.

It is that transcendent reception (protestant though it must also be) of their long experience of isolation and murder which has gone so deeply into the Jewish poetry of place: 'Poet, what of the night in the Hebrew homeland?', asked Uri Zvi Greenberg; and he, a refugee from the Polish pogroms, always amongst the most vicious in Europe before the rise of the Nazis, found that the poetry of the holy land was bound to be an act of endurance, which the history of Jerusalem alone made possible to sustain:

> The trees, few by the door,
> Bend to a forest roar:
> The thunder-bearing clouds
> Are heavy with streaming shrouds.
> The angels of peace guard my children sleeping,
> With the trees lamenting, the heavy rains weeping.

> Outside – City of the Father's tested will,
> His son bound on the demanding hill,
> His fire, touched at first light,
> Burns, unaffected by the rain, still bright:
> It is the fire which burns its price
> Between the pieces of the sacrifice.

> If I by God were told
> As was my Father once, of old,
> 'This do', I would obey – with all my life
> Upon this night of storm and strife,
> While angels of peace guard my children sleeping,
> With the trees lamenting, the heavy rains weeping.

What can equal this glory,
What the zeal of this story,
Life-endowing from that first dawning
On Mount Moriah, to this new morning?
The blood of the covenant sings in the Father's will
To bind on the Temple Mount the offering still.

Outside – Jerusalem: in grief
The Lord's trees, beyond belief,
Cut down by her foes
In every age that comes and goes:
Clouds, pregnant with rain, split with lightning,
Gloomy with thunder, no sign of brightening:
   From the mouth of God, all things transcending,
   This for me is His word, world without ending.

ELEVEN

❀ The Heavenly Jerusalem

The poetry of place and praise sings most eloquently of Jerusalem, and it does so, not only for Jews, but for Muslims and Christians as well. But where is Jerusalem? Obviously at the centre of the earth in an earlier age, and at the centre of conflict for the more modern temperament. But is Jerusalem on earth at all? At least as much of its poetry has seen it as the place – if such it be – of our eternal home; and always, therefore, on the edge of metaphor, because God is not confined to any place, in heaven or on earth, not even to the places of his particular occasion. When Judah haLevi longed to return to Jerusalem, he was longing for much more than a tour of the Holy Land:

> Lord, where shall I find you?
> Your place is high and concealed.
> But where shall I fail to find you?
> Every place is your glory revealed.
>
> You are found in the depth of our mind,
> Yet you order the furthest extreme;
> Those at hand you protect as a tower,
> Those afar, in their trust, you redeem.
>
> The cherubim serve as a throne,
> Yet you dwell far above every place,
> The spheres of the sky are too small,
> The Temple defective of space.
>
> Far above, far exalted on high,
> You are nearer than body to soul,
> We know you the maker of all,
> Creating, sustaining, the whole.
>
> Who will not fall at your feet?
> The yoke of your kingdom we bear;

Who will not call on your name?
All life is sustained by your care.

To you I have longed to come near,
With you I am yearning to be:
In my quest I found you on the road
Already close searching for me.

I gaze on your wonders with awe –
Who can say you are hid from our sight?
Without voices, the heavens are loud
With the praise of your glory and might.

Can God dwell with those who are dust,
Who are shadows not knowing the sun?
Yet here you have built you a home
In a glory out-splendoured by none.

A tumult of life on the earth,
In the sky, in the sea, on the land,
Raises you in the net of its praise
While carried by you in your hand.

This transferring of Jerusalem into the future made it, in
the Christian case, a virtual synonym for heaven. It evoked
a cascade of superb Latin hymns, from at least the fourth
century onward – many of which were translated into
English by J. M. Neale, whose skill produced new treasures
out of old: '*Chorus novae Jerusalem*' – 'Ye choirs of new
Jerusalem'; '*O bona patria*' – 'For thee, O dear, dear country';
'*Jerusalem luminosa*' – 'Light's abode, celestial Salem'; '*Urbs
beata Jerusalem*' – 'Blessed city, heavenly Salem'; and part of
Bernard of Cluny's *Hora novissima*, '*Urbs Sion aurea*':

Jerusalem the golden,
    With milk and honey blest,
Beneath thy contemplation
    Sink heart and voice opprest.
I know not, O I know not,
    What social joys are there,
What radiancy of glory,
    What light beyond compare.

They stand, those halls of Sion,
　　Conjubilant with song,
And bright with many an Angel,
　　And all the Martyr throng;
The Prince is ever in them,
　　The daylight is serene,
The pastures of the blessed
　　Are decked in glorious sheen.

There is the throne of David,
　　And there, from care released,
The song of them that triumph,
　　The shout of them that feast;
And they who, with their Leader,
　　Have conquered in the fight,
For ever and for ever
　　Are clad in robes of white.

O sweet and blessed country,
　　Shall I ever see thy face?
O sweet and blessed country,
　　Shall I ever win thy grace?
Exult, O dust and ashes!
　　The Lord shall be thy part:
His only, his for ever,
　　Thou shalt be, and thou art!

From this transformation, it is not surprising that Jerusalem became even more diversely metaphorical. In Torquato Tasso's *Gerusalemme Liberata*, it became an excuse for wild flights of romantic fancy. But in the poetry of William Blake, Jerusalem became a powerful metaphor of protest and change:

I will not cease from mental fight,
Nor shall my sword sleep in my hand,
Till we have built Jerusalem
In England's green and pleasant land.

But in the long poem, 'Jerusalem: the Emanation of the Giant Albion', the image of Jerusalem is far more intricately interwoven into London (p. *ix*) and Britain as Blake envisaged them in their spiritual redemption and atonement:

So Los spoke. But when he saw blue death in Albion's
    feet
Again he join'd the Divine Body, following merciful,
While Albion fled more indignant, revengeful covering
His face and bosom with petrific hardness, and his hands
And feet, lest any should enter his bosom and embrace
His hidden heart; his Emanation wept and trembled
    within him,
Uttering not his jealousy but hiding it as with
Iron and steel, dark and opake, with clouds and tempests
    brooding;
His strong limbs shudder'd upon his mountains high and
    dark
Turning from Universal Love, petrific as he went,
His cold against the warmth of Eden rag'd with loud
Thunders of deadly war (the fever of the human soul)
Fires and clouds of rolling smoke! but mild, the Saviour
    follow'd him,
Displaying the Eternal Vision, the Divine Similitude,
In loves and tears of brothers, sisters, sons, fathers and
    friends,
Which if Man ceases to behold, he ceases to exist,

Saying, 'Albion! Our wars are wars of life, & wounds of
    love
    With intellectual spears, & long winged arrows of
        thought.
    Mutual in one another's love and wrath all renewing
    We live as One Man; for contracting our infinite
        senses
    We behold multitude, or expanding, we behold as one,
    As One Man all the Universal Family, and that One
        Man
    We call Jesus the Christ; and he in us, and we in him
    Live in perfect harmony in Eden, the land of life,
    Giving, receiving, and forgiving each other's trespasses.
    He is the Good shepherd, he is the Lord and master,
    He is the Shepherd of Albion, he is all in all,
    In Eden, in the garden of God, and in heavenly
        Jerusalem.

If we have offended, forgive us; take not vengeance
   against us.'

Thus speaking, the Divine Family follow Albion.
I see them in the Vision of God upon my pleasant valleys.

I behold London, a Human awful wonder of God!
He says: 'Return, Albion, return! I give myself for thee.
   My Streets are my Ideas of Imagination.
   Awake Albion, awake! and let us awake up together.
   My Houses are Thoughts: my Inhabitants, Affections,
   The children of my thoughts walking within my
      blood-vessels,
   Shut from my nervous form which sleeps upon the
      verge of Beulah
   In dreams of darkness, while my vegetating blood in
      veiny pipes
   Rolls dreadful thro' the Furnaces of Los and the Mills
      of Satan.
   For Albion's sake and for Jerusalem thy Emanation
   I give myself, and these my brethren give themselves
      for Albion.'

So spoke London, immortal Guardian! I heard in Lambeth's
   shades.
In Felpham I heard and saw the Visions of Albion.
I write in South Molton Street what I both see and hear
In regions of Humanity, in London's opening streets.

In the poetry of Blake, Jerusalem is still connected with the
geography of this earth. But the heavenly Jerusalem, the city
of peace, supplied more powerful images still, whereby the
places of poetry become the metaphors of our desire:

      My soul, there is a country
        Far beyond the stars,
      Where stands a winged sentry
        All skilful in the wars,
      There above noise, and danger
        Sweet peace sits crowned with smiles,
      And one born in a manger
        Commands the beauteous files,

> He is thy gracious friend,
>   And (O my soul awake!)
> Did in pure love descend
>   To die here for thy sake,
> If thou canst get but thither,
>   There grows the flower of peace,
> The rose that cannot whither,
>   Thy fortress and thy ease;
> Leave then thy foolish ranges,
>   For none can thee secure,
> But one who never changes,
>   Thy God, thy life, they cure.

Here poetry has moved far beyond the imagination of heaven as a place: it takes us into the truth which Philo (or at least his translator) expressed in four simple words: *non locus, sed Deus* – 'not a place, but God'. The places of poetry and their idioms point beyond themselves to the final condition of our return and rest:

> Imagine all the heavens above,
> Imagine all the worlds of love,
> Of deva, pitr, atman, soul
> Enticed into Thyself as goal –
> Thyself my golden shore, my crystal sea:
> Be Thou that gate for me, land of sweet liberty,
> Be Western Paradise, and Eden – east
> Of all expulsions from the final feast:
> Be the foundation, the recovered stone,
> Be Thou the place not place but God alone.

TWELVE

❀ *The Place of Death*

The poetry of place has touched with its transforming word virtually every place where humans live. But it can hardly travel, one might suppose, to a place (if place it be) where humans only go but do not return – the place of death, 'the undiscover'd country from whose bourn No traveller returns'. But there at once is the point: the imagination is not barred from an exploration even of the unknown, even of the possibility that the place of death is no place but cool oblivion; or even *if* a place, one where nothing but thin ghosts of memory are the merest shadows of a life on earth. It is a neglected truth that the great and continuing religious traditions, both East and West, had in origin no belief that there will be a worthwhile life after death. In the Jewish Bible, the truth of death is as absolute as it was for Swinburne in his austere lines, that life continues only

> . . . till the night of death
> Severeth our memory from itself
> And us from all.

The Psalms portray Sheol, the primitive grave, as a place truly abhorrent to the living, because in Sheol all connection with the living and with God is cut off. In all religions, the early poetry of death tends to be a poetry, not of speculation about some place of paradise, but of extreme realism about human nature. There is nothing here of an evasive wish-fulfillment which cannot accept the finality of death where we are concerned:

> Man that is born of a woman
>   Is but of few days and full of trouble.
> He comes forth like a flower and is cut down,
>   He flees also as a shadow and continues not . . .
> There is hope for a tree, if it be cut down, that it will
>   sprout again,

> And that the tender branch thereof will not cease.
> Though the root thereof wax old in the earth,
>   And the stock thereof die in the ground,
> Yet through the scent of water it will bud,
>   And bring forth boughs like a plant.
> But man dies and wastes away:
>   He gives up the ghost. And where is he?

In the enduring religious traditions of both East and West, there was (as I have shown in the book, *The Meanings of Death*) no hope that there would be any worthwhile life with God after death. At the most, the dead throw forward into the generations which succeed them nothing more than a memory-trace of themselves – as faint as the thin squeak of a bat in the dark recesses of a cave:

> Hermes then summoned forth the shades of all the suitors.
> He held with both his hands a staff both fair and golden:
> With this he lulls to sleep the eyes of whom he wills,
> While others yet again he wakens from their slumber.
> With this he roused the shades who followed thinly squeaking:
> As bats within the darkness of an awe-inspiring cave
> Squeaking flit about, when one drops off the rock
> Falling from the chain of each one joined to others,
> So these went with him squeaking; and he led them,
> Hermes the Helper, down the dank ways below.

The place of death cannot be other than a stupendous and awe-inspiring darkness – unless illuminated by God, as Vaughan so repeatedly perceived: 'I saw eternity the other night, Like a great ring of pure and endless light'; 'They are all gone into the world of light, And I alone sit lingering here'; 'Wise Nicodemus saw such light As made him know his God by night'; 'I cannot reach it; and my striving eye Dazzles at it, as at eternity'; 'There is in God – some say – A deep, but dazzling darkness'. So it may be. But not even Lazarus has left us any record of what Rilke called 'the unallowed' – that earlier and proleptic harrowing of hell:

One had to bear with the majority –
what they wanted was a sign that screamed:
Martha, though, and Mary – he had dreamed
they would be contented just to see
that he *could*. But not a soul believed him:
'Lord, you've come too late,' said all the crowd.
So to peaceful Nature, though it grieved him,
on he went to do the unallowed.
Asked them, eyes half-shut, his body glowing
with anger, 'Where's the grave?' Tormentedly.
And to them it seemed his tears were flowing,
as they thronged behind him, curiously.
As he walked, the thing seemed monstrous to him,
childish, horrible experiment:
then there suddenly went flaming through him
such an all-consuming argument
against their life, their death, their whole collection
of separations made by them alone,
all his body quivered with rejection
as he gave out hoarsely 'Raise the stone'.
Someone shouted that the corpse was stinking
(buried now four days ago) – but He
stood erect, brim-full of that unblinking,
mounting gesture, that so painfully
lifted up his hand (no hand was ever
raised so slowly, so immeasurably),
till it stood there, shining in the gloom.
There it slowly, clawingly contracted:
what if all the dead should be attracted
upwards, through that syphon of a tomb,
where a pallid chrysalidal thing
was writhing up from where it had been lying? –
But it stood alone (no more replying),
and they saw vague, unidentifying
Life compelled to give it harbouring.

But then, of course, in the very narrative of contradiction,
we realize at once that the place of death is not some
speculation about the geography of a condition which
would have to be as much bereft of space as it is of time – *non*

locus sed Deus. As one of Hartley Coleridge's sonnets ends:

> Think not the faith by which the just shall live
> Is a dead creed, a map correct of heaven,
> Far less a feeling fond and fugitive,
> A thoughtless gift withdrawn as soon as given.
> It is an affirmation and an act
> That bids eternal truth be present fact.

In that context, the place of death is the place where death occurs – the place which it is the work of poetry to open up to opportunity. The poetry of the place of our death carries in its hands the accumulated meaning of the life which has preceded it (even if that 'meaning' seems nothing more than some theatre of the absurd); and it mediates the nature of that life's transition into whatever possibility there still may be (even if that possibility is nothing more than Lawrence's 'long journey towards oblivion').

Religions have not evaded the possibility of oblivion. But they have not refused, either, to explore the possibility that what has been secured of truth, in unmistakeable effect, during this brief transience of a life, may be continued and sustained beyond it. Those who have not experienced the effect are inclined to look on, from afar, and mock. Whether they are wise to do so, time will not tell. As it is, the religious poetry of the place of our death is more often concerned with transition than with description, and with the support of the dying in the ultimate moments of truth. So it is in Varanasi, Banaras, which Hindus call Kashi, the city of light. If a Hindu makes his last pilgrimage to die there, the accumulations of karma, which might otherwise have brought him back to another birth in some other form of appearance, will be lifted away by Śiva, and he will move directly to *moksa*, to release:

> Where else but here do creatures fly
> So simply into freedom?
> A mere abandoning of body;
> No great denials, no obsequious gifts,
> No lavish sacrifice
> As all elsewhere attempt.

> Here in Kashi the gift is simple:
> Give up the body to the fire.
> Even the yogi with a mind controlled
> Who wanders on from life to life
> Will here in Kashi reach the goal
> Simply by dying.

For it is in Kashi that the guru who teaches the sacred, liberating formula, the mantra, is not some human; it is Śiva himself. He it is who whispers in the ear of the dying person the 'carrying across' – the taraka – mantra, the ferryboat mantra of the great crossing over.

But something like it is true for all religious traditions. Among the American Indians, the place of death is the whole world as a place of life, through a constant cycle of return – 'give up the body' indeed:

> I have killed the deer.
> I have crushed the grasshopper
> And the plants he feeds upon.
> I have cut through the heart
> Of trees growing old and straight.
> I have taken fish from water
> And birds from the sky.
> In my life I have needed death
> So that my life can be.
> When I die I must give life
> To what has nourished me.
> The earth receives my body
> And gives it to the plants
> And to the caterpillars
> To the birds
> And to the coyotes
> Each in its own turn so that
> The circle of life is never broken.

So the poetry of place in relation to death then becomes supremely important in supporting or sustaining the dead as they make their transition from one state to another. The support and assurance may be very simple, as in the prayer of committal recorded by John Mbiti in Africa:

The gates of the underworld are closed.
Closed are the gates.

The spirits of the dead are thronging together
Like swarming mosquitoes in the evening,
like swarming mosquitoes.
Like swarms of mosquitoes dancing in the evening,
When the night has turned black, entirely black,
When the sun has sunk, has sunk below,
when the night has turned black
the mosquitoes are swarming
like whirling leaves, dead leaves in the wind.

Dead leaves in the wind,
they wait for him who will come
for him who will come and will say:
'Come' to the one and 'Go' to the other,
And God will be with his children.
And God will be with his children.

The mosquitoes of Africa are displaced in Tibet by the
Bodhisattvas, those who are fully enlightened but who
refuse to rest in that peace until they have helped every
suffering entity to find the same truth. The invocations to
them continue even when the body of the one for whom the
prayer is made is most clearly lifeless:

The saints and holy ones, having peaceful minds
That have passed beyond harmful thoughts and
Who have totally crushed stains of attachment,
Will bring but goodness and joy to you.

The spiritual masters who direct beings
To the path of ultimate freedom
And reveal every truth
Will bring but goodness and joy to you.

The teachers, supports of living beings,
Who for the sake of the world
Guide seekers to the land of bliss,
Will bring but goodness and joy to you.

The saints, with hearts of love,
Regard each and every living being
As a mother does her only child;
They will bring but goodness and joy to you.

The Bodhisattvas, who act as a home and a friend
To help and support every living being
Circling in the sea of becoming,
Will bring but goodness and joy to you.

They who appear as spiritual warriors
To bestow everything sublime
And fulfill all hopes of the world
Will bring but goodness and joy to you.

Those whose very birth caused
Earth and forests to quiver in awe
And living beings to weep in bliss
Will bring but goodness and joy to you.

They who when they passed to enlightenment
Caused the six worlds to shake
And evil Mara to be filled with anxiety
Will bring but goodness and joy to you.

They who turn the Wheel of Dharma
And speak the four noble truths
By manifesting as a Muni, a sage,
Will bring but goodness and joy to you.

They who with the power of beauty
Tumble the wrong views of sophists
And tame the wild minds of barbarians
Will bring but goodness and joy to you.

May the Enlightened Ones bring you every joy
And every goodness of men and gods.
May they bring you happiness surpassing
That of the most powerful divinity.

May the Enlightened Ones, who have merits
And thoughts more sublime than all the gods,
Fulfill for you this very day
Your each and every hope for goodness.

May the Enlightened Ones bring joy to mankind,
May they bring harmony to the animal kingdom,
May they bring the world to the way of truth
And in future may they hold us in happiness.

May they bring joy day and night
And during dawn and dusk as well.
May they encourage every happiness by
Imparting the joy of spiritual knowledge.

May they bring joy day and night
And at noon and midnight as well.
May they give us every happiness
By showing the ways by which evil is purified.

It is not much other for the Christian soul as it begins its journey into life:

Go forth upon your journey, Christian soul,
In the name of God the Father, who created you;
In the name of Jesus Christ, who died for you;
In the name of the Holy Spirit, who sustains you still:
May your place be this day in peace, and your dwelling place in Sion;
May the angels lead you into paradise,
May the martyrs greet you and lead you into the holy city of Jerusalem;
May a choir of angels welcome you;
And there, where Lazarus is poor no longer, may you rest in peace.

May this be true for us, that we may, as John Donne put it,

awake as Jacob did, and say as Jacob said, 'Surely the Lord is in this place', and, 'This is no other but the house of God, and the gate of heaven.' And into that gate they shall enter, and in that house they shall dwell, where there shall be no Cloud nor Sun, no darkness nor dazzling, but one equal light, no noise nor silence, but one equal music, no fears nor hopes, but one equal possession, no foes nor friends, but an equal communion and Identity, no ends nor beginnings, but one equal eternity. Keep us, Lord, so awake in the duties of our Callings, that we may thus sleep in thy Peace, and wake in thy glory. . . .

❧ Conclusion

The poetry of place may be descriptive or nostalgic or angry at desecration or compelled by beauty – or by many other engagements of the human imagination in the occasions of space. But it becomes another voice when it arises from the fact that people live religiously in two places at once. They live with their feet on the ground, in places as they are; but they live also in places as they might be in the horizons of hope – though in contrast, sometimes of fear. The places where we live look entirely different when they are invaded by the signals of a particular religious imagination. It is that added value which transforms the presentation of place into a real presence. Wheat becomes orient and the children moving jewels, and not just for Traherne (p. 14):

> Because I could not stop for Death –
> He kindly stopped for me –
> The Carriage held but just Ourselves –
> And Immortality.
>
> We slowly drove – He knew no haste
> And I had put away
> My labor and my leisure too,
> For His Civility –
>
> We passed the School, where Children strove
> At Recess – in the Ring –
> We passed the Fields of Gazing Grain –
> We passed the Setting Sun –
>
> Or rather – He passed Us –
> The dews drew quivering and chill –
> For only Gossamer, my Gown –
> My Tippet – only Tulle –

> We paused before a House that seemed
> A swelling of the Ground –
> The Roof was scarcely visible –
> The Cornice – in the Ground –
>
> Since then – 'tis Centuries – and yet
> Feels shorter than the Day
> I first surmised the Horses' Heads
> Were toward Eternity.

The religious poetry of place makes connection between the two conditions, of the existing place and of our possible future state, of the reality and the aspiration. It is, in more technical jargon, a realized eschatology. It is by no means a lapse into naive projection, although of course it may be; examples of that are not difficult to find:

> On the margin of the river
> Washing up its silver spray,
> We will walk and worship ever,
> All the happy golden day,
>
> Ere we reach the shining river,
> Lay we every burden down;
> Grace our spirits will deliver,
> And provide a robe and crown.

The emotional power of such hymns as that – 'Shall we gather at the river?' – is immense, above all for those in a condition of slavery. But it rests on the level of description because it settles for a literal correspondence between the biblical image and the imagined future state. Since that future state can neither be known nor described, the more enduring religious poetry of place is constantly struggling with the way in which the horizon of human hope – and fear – affects our experience of the present place and time. It wrestles with the connection between the present circumstance and the condition toward which the one located in that circumstance is moving.

But the images of that connection are drawn, very often, from the past. Here, at least, we can recognize the ground on which we stand. There is a conversation between the old and new Jerusalem, between the buddha-nature in every place and the no-place of nirvana, between Kashi and Siva, which the poetry of place can mediate. So, not surprisingly, the religious poetry of place moves backward in time as well as forward, making further connections between space and significance: both past and future are brought into the present, and are realized in the power of words to create that toward which they point. The places of religious poetry are lifted out of chronology by the meanings they have borne in the past and may yet bear now, albeit in transfigured form. This means that such poetry is not a mere archaeology of time, an attempt to rescue something of the past before it disappears into oblivion. That attempt at rescue was, in contrast, exactly the purpose of the great antiquarians of the seventeenth century. When William Camden set out, in the early seventeenth century, to provide 'a Chorographical Description of the most flourishing Kingdomes, England, Scotland, and Ireland, and the Ilands adjoyning, out of the Depth of Antiquitie', he promised

> that I would restore antiquity to Britaine, and Britain to his antiquity, which was, as I understood, that I would renew ancientrie, enlighten obscuritie, cleare doubts, and recall home veritie by way of recovery, which the negligence of writers and credulitie of the common sort had in a manner proscribed and utterly banished from amongst us.

When he visited Cockersand Abbey on the Lancashire coast, the ruins were already threatened by the encroaching tides, and he was more impressed by the dangers, as real now as then, of the mud-flats of Morecambe Bay:

> Heere along the sea shore, you may see in many places, heapes of sand, whereupon they powre water, untill it gather a saltish humor which afterwards with turfes they boile untill it be white salt. There be also here uncertaine sands not to be trusted, but ready to catch and swallow, they call them *Quick-sands*, so dangerous for travailours, whiles at a low water when tide is past they seeke to goe the nerest way, that they had neede to take

very good heed least in going a foote (I use *Sidonius* his wordes) they suffer not shipwracke and be cast away on the land; but especially about the mouth of *Cocar*, where, as it were, in a field of *Syrts* or *Quick-sands*, *Cokar sand Abby*, an Abbay not long since of the Cluniack monkes, built by Ranulph *de Meschines*, but open to the violence of windes, stoode betweene the mouthes of *Cocar* or *Lune* or *Lone* and hath a bleake prospect into the wide Irish sea.

But for the religious poetry of place, there will always be more to the journey backward through time – that 'envious and ravenous enemy', as Camden called it – than the rescue of items from oblivion. Nearly four hundred years later, we can go, as he did, to Cockersand, and we can still see the last fragile hold of that past still eloquent – the Chapter House, now used as a barn, standing resistant against the gale:

Across the flat, where caravans and cars
Thread their persistent way toward the shore,
In furthest desolate uncivil solitude
They set, those Cluniacs, a wall against the sea.
The sea returns, no more the cowl
Tracing obedience across a winter sky.
A single thorn laid parallel to earth
Is eloquent of estuary storm:
O vast expansive transience of the sky,
Hinting of consequence and human worth,
The very graves are gone:
The flesh, the sinews, the eroded bones
Are drawn by crumbling earth into the tide.
The space where stones were set against the storm
Fell into the sea.
The earth surrenders: only secure
The chapter house of square and single stone:
Pragmatic farmers saved it for a barn;
And there, where herded cattle ruminate at night,
By day the herded tourist snuffs around,
Peering on tiptoe through a broken board:
He sees, not mystery opaque with light,
But darkness heavy with the smell of dung.
O vast expansive transience of the sky . . .

A shook kaleidoscope of birds
In shifting pattern falls across the light;
The gulls cry Kyrie where once
A monk fell prostrate in the pledge of loss
To set his life a stone in God's repair.
And now? And now
No sanctus bell, no angelus at noon,
Only the secular clang from off the shore
Where, like a startled goose, an anchored buoy
Raises its bulk above the tide and mud.
Go forth upon your journey, Christian soul,
Soul of this place, go forth:
Be born again in other stone and life.
And here, where angels touch the world in peace,
Give birth to other hope in alien clay.

It follows that a poet may create a religious poetry of place by standing deliberately on hallowed ground, as John Betjeman so often did, or as Elizabeth Jennings does, in 'San Paolo fuori le Mura, Rome'

It is the stone makes stillness here, I think
There could not be so much of silence if
The columns were not set there rank on rank,
For silence needs a shape in which to sink
And stillness needs these shadows for its life.

My darkness throws so little space before
My body where it stands, and yet my mind
Needs the large echoing churches and the roar
Of streets outside its own calm place to find
Where the soft doves of peace withdraw, withdraw.

The alabaster windows here permit
Only suggestions of the sun to slide
Into the church and make a glow in it;
The battering daylight leaps at large outside
Though what slips here through jewels seems most fit.

And here one might in his discovered calm
Feel the great building draw away from him,
His head bent closely down upon his arm,

With all the sun subsiding to a dim
Past-dreamt-of peace, a kind of coming home.

For me the senses still have their full sway
Even where prayer comes quicker than an act.
I cannot quite forget the blazing day,
The alabaster windows or the way
The light refuses to be called abstract.

But a religious place does not automatically produce
religious poetry. Thus Wordsworth stood in a place of
obvious religious association and wrote his sonnet, 'The
Inside of King's College Chapel, Cambridge':

Tax not the royal saint with vain expense,
With ill-matched aims the Architect who planned –
Albeit labouring for a scanty band
Of white-robed scholars only – this immense
And glorious Work of fine intelligence!
Give all thou canst; high Heaven rejects the lore
Of nicely-calculated less or more;
So deemed the man who fashioned forth the sense
These lofty pillars, spread that branching roof
Self-poised, and scooped into ten thousand cells,
Where light and shade repose, where music dwells
Lingering – and wandering on as loth to die;
Like thoughts whose very sweetness yieldeth proof
That they were born for immortality.

These reflections are clearly very different from those of
Charles Causley when, 150 years later, he stood in the same
place and heard a comparable music:

When to the music of Byrd or Tallis,
　The ruffed boys singing in the blackened stalls,
The candles lighting the small bones on their faces,
　The Tudors stiff in marble on the walls,

There comes to evensong Elizabeth or Henry
　Rich with brocade, pearl, golden lilies, at the altar,
The scarlet lions leaping on their bosoms,
　Pale royal hands fingering the crackling psalter,

Henry is thinking of his lute and of backgammon,
 Elizabeth follows the waving song, the mystery,
Proud in her red wig and green jewelled favours;
 They sit in their white lawn sleeves, as cool as history.

Here the ironies of religious dedication take us at once into
a different world. But that is simply to emphasize that religious poetry does not come into being simply because it
has to do with a religious subject-matter – in this case, a
religious place. It depends on a willingness to allow the
appropriate and relevant symbols to speak for themselves;
otherwise, the emotion may still be extremely powerful,
but it will stop short at the boundary of its own refusals.
Alexander Morin, who used to describe himself insistently
as 'a dogmatic scientific materialist', remembered years later
how he was affected by his first visit to King's College Chapel:

> I was a young and ardent pilgrim to the holy places of
> American literary and intellectual tradition, and greatly
> excited by the extraordinary experiences I was having. . .
> The chapel by itself was enough to fill me with awe, but
> in addition I arrived at Evensong, just as the choristers
> were beginning the vesper service. Row upon row of
> young boys in white surplices, their fresh faces radiant in
> the light that filtered through the gothic traceries,
> singing sweet songs with the voices of angels. There I
> stood – that worldly-wise atheist from the tough-minded
> west side of Chicago – and I broke down. I found myself
> literally shaking, with tears streaming down my face, in
> the grip of emotions that I did not understand and could
> not control. After a few moments I realized that a man
> standing nearby was watching me closely. He was
> dressed in clerical robes, perhaps those of a deacon of the
> church, and when he caught my eye, he came closer and
> said in quiet voice, 'Isn't it wonderful to come so close to
> the glory and beauty of God?' This was such an alien
> notion to me that at first I had no response to make. But,
> as I listened to the music and looked around the chapel, I
> realized what it really meant. 'No,' I said, 'but isn't it
> wonderful to come so close to the glory and beauty of
> humanity!'

Here, as always, the issue is one of perception. The occasions of absolute beauty are so stunning and unexpected that they come to us truly as an unexpected gift. We may of course accept the gift with gratitude, as Alexander Morin did, and leave it at that. We may even stand in an obviously religious place and feel nothing but anger and rejection – as did Iain Colley, standing before the tomb of the Reverend John Clarke Hayden, in Chalfont St Giles churchyard:

> The priest-in-ordinary rots in state:
> No marble chips that make the grass ashamed
> For him, simply a ponderous stone box
> Like a Victorian domestic headache.
> Railings protect him from the casual ghoul,
> Or else restrain his energetic ghost.
> Here in this graveyard I conjure Clarke Hayden
> Alive, more live than all the recent dead.
> Between these quiet corpses and the children
> Crossing the meadow for secular instruction,
> My mind is captured by a vicar's bones.
> Pray for me, Clarke Hayden, damn your soul,
> Pray I may keep the ache of modernism,
> Life and cheat and doubt and always escape
> Your nightmare certainty. Nineteen centuries
> Of error you carried like your sermon-notes
> To dump them on my brain. Decomposed
> Into muck, you still offer me a fight
> And make me blaspheme in the bitter air
> And stamp the grass round your sarcophagus.

But the assumption of error – 'nineteen centuries of error' – in every age before that of modernity (modernism being in any case a highly relative term) is itself an elementary error. In contrast to *that* nightmare certainty, we may begin to suspect that where there is a gift, there is One who gives it – One who bestows upon us the transfigurations of occasion or place. There is certainly no compulsion to see the world in this way. But it is by no means abject to do so, as Freud and Marx – and many of our contemporaries – have supposed that it is. On the contrary, it allows us to take the measure of our giftedness as being indeed a product of both chance and necessity, but as having also the independent guarantee of its eternal worth discernible within the nature and quality of its own uncontrived experience. We are returned once more to Hopkins – albeit in this instance recognizing the absolute demand evoked by the beauty, not of place, but of human presence:

> To what serves mortal beauty/—dangerous; does set danc-
> ing blood—the O-seal-that so/feature, flung prouder
>   form
> Than Purcell tune lets tread to?/See: it does this: keeps
>   warm
> Men's wits to the things that are;/what good means —
>   where a glance
> Master more may than gaze,/gaze out of countenance.

It is not necessarily peace that breaks out of that presence: it may be war – or grief or emptiness, as the poetry of R. S. Thomas has repeatedly insisted. Yet still it will be a religious poetry of place that goes down into the grave and seeks, not the 'solutions' of wishful thinking, but the weight of truth which the place will bear – even 'In Church':

> Often I try
> To analyse the quality
> Of its silences. Is this where God hides
> From my searching? I have stopped to listen,
> After the few people have gone,
> To the air recomposing itself
> For vigil. It has waited like this
> Since the stones grouped themselves about it.
> These are the hard ribs
> Of a body that our prayers have failed
> To animate. Shadows advance
> From their corners to take possession
> Of places the light held
> For an hour. The bats resume
> Their business. The uneasiness of the pews
> Ceases. There is no other sound
> In the darkness but the sound of a man
> Breathing, testing his faith

On emptiness, nailing his questions
One by one to an untenanted cross.

We confer on places the power of their presence, but we
receive from them the capacity to see them at all in those
transcendent ways. The places which evoke poetry are
exactly that gift from God when they invade us with the
independence of their value and of their judgement, when
they are instantiations of those absolute values of truth, of
goodness, of beauty – even 'in Church':

Six centuries now have gone
Since, one by one,
These stones were laid,
And in air's vacancy
This beauty made.

They who thus reared them
Their long rest have won;
Ours now this heritage –
To guard, preserve, delight in, brood upon;
And in these transitory fragments scan
The immortal longings in the soul of Man.

It is for this reason that the twentieth century has been one
of the greatest ages of religious poetry – at exactly the time
when we have been assured that the sea of faith is going
out, and that belief has become impossible in the reality of
One who gives and who sustains what he has given. But it is
God who still insists on his presence in the places which
arrest us by their power. It is not that God can ever be *seen*
directly in the places of his occasion. It is, rather, that when
we look upon them, we begin, if we are wise, to realize that
God is.

That is why the connections between earth and heaven
are still to be made by poets, provided they do not assume
that the images of either have been exhausted in the waste-
lands of scientism at one extreme or of fundamentalism at
another. We live in two places at once, in heaven as on
earth, on earth as in heaven. It is the poet who can make
them at one:

Place is the focus. What is the language
Of stones? I do not mean
As emblems of patience, philosophers' hopes
Or as the astrological tangents
One may assemble, draw out subjectively
From a lapidary inertia. Only we
Are inert. Stones act, like pictures, by remaining
Always the same, unmoving, waiting on presence
Unpredictable in absence, inhuman
In a human dependence, a physical
Point of contact, for a movement not physical
And on a track of force, the milestone
Between two infinities. Stones are like deaths.
They uncover limits.

❧ Acknowledgements and Sources

The author and SPCK are grateful to individuals and publishers for their permission to reproduce copyright material in this book. Unattributed verse and translations are by the author. Every effort has been made to trace and acknowledge copyright holders. Information on any omissions should be communicated to the SPCK, who will make full acknowledgement in future editions of this book.

Introduction
'The fields from Islington . . .': from William Blake, 'Jerusalem'.
'The blank lack of any charm . . .': from 'After a Romantic Day'.
'There's a certain Slant of Light . . .': in T. H. Johnson, ed., *The Complete Poems of Emily Dickinson*, London: Faber and Faber, 1970, p. 118.
'By this time . . .': J. Bunyan, *The Pilgrim's Progress*.

1. Remembered Places
'I remember, I remember . . .': Thomas Hood.
'I wandered . . .': W. Wordsworth.
'Shades of the prison-house . . .': W. Wordsworth, 'Ode to Immortality'.
'I am sad . . .': W. Wordsworth, *The Prelude*, Bk. V, ll.545–52.
'Here must we pause . . .': op.cit., ll.584–605.
'No doubt my poetry . . .': from C. Phillips, ed., *Gerard Manley Hopkins: Selected Letters*, Oxford: Clarendon Press, 1990, p. 117.
'To use familiar examples . . .': W. Lynch, *Christ and Apollo: the Dimensions of the Literary Imagination*, New York: New American Library, 1963, p. 21.
'By grasping . . .': *Commentary* tr. A. B. Wolter.
'Towery City . . .': 'Duns Scotus's Oxford', in W. H. Gardner and N. H. MacKenzie, eds, *The Poems of Gerard Manley Hopkins*, Oxford: Oxford University Press, 1970, p. 79.
'The world is charged . . .': 'The Grandeur of God', op.cit., p. 66.
'I am in Ireland . . .': 'To seem the stranger lies my lot', op.cit., p. 101.
'I remember a house . . .': 'In the Valley of the Elwy', op.cit., pp. 67ff.

2. China and Tao
'You look at it . . .': *Tao-te Ching*, xiv.
'The Tao that can be described . . .': *Tao-te Ching*, i.
'Always non-existent . . .': *Tao-te Ching*, ii.